O9-ABE-620

YOUNG OUTSIDERS

YOUNG
OUTSIDERS

A Study of Alternative Communities

BY

Richard Mills

Pantheon Books
A Division of Random House, New York

FIRST AMERICAN EDITION

Copyright © 1973 by Institute of Community Studies

All rights reserved under International and Pan-American Copyright Conventions. Published in the United States by Pantheon Books, a division of Random House, Inc., New York. Originally published in Great Britain by Routledge & Kegan Paul, London.

Library of Congress Cataloging in Publication Data

Mills, Richard, 1945–
Young Outsiders.

Bibliography: pp. 200–201
1. Hippies—London. I. Title.
HQ799.8.G72L66 1973   301.44'94'09421   73–5929
ISBN 0-394-48723-0

Manufactured in the United States of America.

CONTENTS

PREFACE
TO THE AMERICAN EDITION

The mood and outlook of this book are English, but the subject
is in some ways too American to require much introduction for
readers in the United States. Although the lives of a few dozen
hippies in London in the summer of 1970 may seem so circum-
scribed in their concerns as to be of no more than parochial interest, they were part of a brief but almost world-wide current of
feeling and expression, which found in America much of its
original impetus and some of its most compelling forms. The
people in this study were as aware of this link as its author. Indeed
they were a living testimony to it, for most of them were at some
time transfixed by the galvanizing myths about the Flower Power
hippies of California. To the detached American observer, able to
follow the detail of such events at closer hand, the connection of
these myths to reality may well have seemed slight, but for thousands of young people half a world away they had, and have
retained, their own important kind of truth.

Not only myth links the people in this study to their trans-
atlantic contemporaries. About the protest generation of the sixties
there was a place-less ecumenicalism, closer to the trans-national
networks of the sciences and technologies than to the more traditional communities of place. Categories of culture and citizenship
came to mean little to them. My English informants could feel as
much the outsider and stranger in the streets of London as if suddenly transported to New York or Boston, Moscow or Tokyo.
There was no place that was home to them. This superficial ecumenicalism also signalled a deeper identity of values and outlook
which extended to the particular subject of this book. The search
for some kind of intensified experience, and the special sense of
wholeness and identity which it was claimed could be glimpsed

through it, did not spring from some specifically English setting, but was rather a temporary response to advanced industrial civilization by that common humanity to which hippies appealed beyond national identities.

To suggest that this ubiquitous theme may endow the lives of a few dozen young English people with relevance for America, or at least interest for Americans, is not to deny the critical differences of culture and experience which separate my informants from their American counterparts. Most of these are too obvious in the pages that follow for me to need to do more than alert the reader to their presence. There is, however, one difference of origin and form that I should mention explicitly, for it seems in part responsible for the different fates that counter-cultural movements currently find in Britain and America.

While the historical precursors of the English hippies are to be found in the Romantics and the Bohemians, their American counterparts have stronger historical parallels with the multitude of chiliastic bands whose search for the millennium has coloured so much of American history. This different origin reflects recurring differences of temper and cast of mind between moral rebels from one side of the Atlantic to the other. If the British political tradition was, and hopefully still is, a dialogue between civilized men which could lead nowhere but to compromise, this was one game from which English hippies felt they could stand aside. From beginning to end they were resolutely committed to playfulness, inconsequence and irresponsibility, holding their moral values aloof from the everyday political world. By comparison the spirit of America, and particularly her political tradition, always appears, from this side of the Atlantic at least, both more idealistic and more pragmatic. This regularly leads her moral rebels to fuse their commitments of conscience and politics and to attempt to build a worldly mansion for their ethical values by the espousal of absolute political goals. However much American hippies overtly scorned conventional politics, many were finally drawn down this path. The resulting linkage of the ethical and the political has often given to the American hippie movement a puritan vein of which the reader will find little reflection in this book. He will see English hippies cultivating an amused detachment from the British political inheritance where at heart the American hippies were grieving deeply for the American dream.

It is in keeping with this difference that the world-wide movement to which the people in this book subscribed should have found a different fate in America than in Britain. Whereas in America much of the ethical protest which hippies originally represented was channelled into specific political commitments, in Britain the traditional separation of the ethical and the political meant that the explosive potential of the Youth Revolt of the 1960s was almost entirely contained. This book is about two small groups in that 'substratum of outcasts and outsiders, the exploited and persecuted of other races and other colours, the unemployed and unemployable' in which Marcuse saw the potential for political liberation. Yet among these people the reader will see all but the most politically conscious contenting themselves with an alienation from the dominant political movements and issues of the day, their isolation endorsed by the traditional pluralism of British political life. But though their paths have been different, their ultimate destinies have been similar, and whether it is better for movements of protest and revolt to exhaust themselves in cathartic conflict or to decay in isolation remains an open question.

If this book were primarily an attempt to chronicle the rise and fall of social movements and their significant dimensions I would have had to explore such differences in greater detail. But I was less concerned with what was socially viable than with what was humanly bearable. As a consequence the book is more concerned with the emotional springs of attachment to certain values and ideas than with their social and political implications. It is an exploration of the private experience of a few people of no special distinction who would themselves eschew the suggestion of any personal importance or political significance. At this level differences between Britain and America in the intellectual source and social context of ethical protest are insignificant. The level of the individual is not only the most particular but also the most general, for it alone is identifiable with that common humanity whose fate in advanced industrial society will hardly admit of British and American variants.

Such an approach no doubt has limitations, but it has at least one advantage besides freeing the author from the need to busy himself with the endless detail of supposedly important political and social events which were known to few and influenced even fewer. With this subject at least, it allows him the comfort of a more hopeful conclusion than might otherwise have been possible. Movements of protest and reform can sometimes succeed when the evidence of superficial social and political events suggests only ugly and bitter failure. It can sometimes happen that members of the silent majority come half-consciously to see in the values and perceptions of the rebels some identity with their own unsung and even unspoken aspirations, and this knowledge can gradually inform and guide at least part of their silence. In the social climate of contemporary England I see some slight evidence that something of this may be happening. The reader may find some slight hint of whether it is happening in America from his own reaction to the perceptions, values and behavior of the people this book describes.

ACKNOWLEDGMENTS

In the course of this study I have accumulated many debts. The largest is to Michael Young and Peter Willmott. The study grew out of my participation in the earlier stages of their study of family, work and leisure in the London Metropolitan Region, and I have drawn heavily on information and ideas I accumulated then, much of it deriving from them. They have since been unfailingly helpful. My thanks are also due to the Centre for Environmental Studies whose support for recent Institute work enabled this part of it to be undertaken.

Kristin Mann, Sheila Morley, Michael Von Haag and Martin Walker made diverse and important contributions to the early stages of the research. Jointly and severally they introduced me to people, places and issues with which I was unfamiliar; joined in parts of the interviewing and field-work; and discussed my rudimentary ideas.

Within the Institute itself Wyn Tucker has been a source of continuing practical support. As the draft of the book passed through the various revisions, it profited from comments by Peter Marris, Roger Mitton, Jim Richardson and Martin Walker.

Comments from David Donnison, Director of the Centre for Environmental Studies, proved particularly helpful in encouraging me to try to turn the book from a personal description and interpretation into one which had a chance of being of some use and interest to others, particularly those concerned with policy.

I would like to record my gratitude to several friends whose contribution though indirect has been important: John Breach, Catherine McAllister, Norman Pratt, Lucy Webster and Christopher Wright. Catherine Mills's contribution to seeing the book to fruition went far beyond typing the final manuscript.

YOUNG OUTSIDERS

I
INTRODUCTION

The beggars realise that you are just searching, that you haven't got anything and they lay off you, except perhaps the little kids wouldn't. But you just smile. If you feel like giving, you give; and that's nice—it's nice to have an opportunity to give. And it's nice to have an opportunity to see life and death—in the real. You don't see them here. People die in their little apartments, and get trundled off in the night in their little cars, and there's a banging and shutting of doors and a sound of weeping in the distance. And you can't get hold of the real things.

Judy is a young American girl who for several years has made London her home. With her English friends she sits talking late into the night in one of the small dark flats from which they move on every few months, less often because of neighbours' complaints than because of their own restlessness. She would be labelled by her contemporaries, and more particularly by her elders and the popular press that serves them, as a 'hippie', a 'drop-out' or a member of the 'underground'; labels she would less willingly use herself. In the summer of 1970 she would probably have labelled herself a 'head' or a 'freak' to catch the spirit of one moment in the life of the moral rebellion of contemporary youth. Judy is one of a cast of some fifty people in their late teens or early twenties who in this book play supporting parts to the thirty people on whose lives it mainly focuses. These eighty or so people were seen in a series of interviews carried out in London in 1970.[1]

There is nothing very special about the person or the time or the place. The scene could be reproduced any number of times within Central London alone, and particularly in the area centred upon Ladbroke Grove and Notting Hill Gate. The subject of the conversation that evening—journeys to Morocco or to Afghanistan, India and Nepal—is equally familiar. To have 'made the East', or at least summered in Morocco, has replaced the Grand Tour of European cities as the entrée to the great world. It reflects a recurrent motif of the contemporary mutiny of youth: rejection of their own advanced industrial society in favour of those African and Asian cultures their fathers not long ago regarded as 'primitive' and 'simple'. These words of the fathers which were once used pejoratively now seem to embody, for the children, some sense of naturalness and wholesomeness.

The flight to the East is a strange and evocative act, and in many ways representative of the behaviour and values that this study tries to describe and explain. It may therefore serve as a point of departure for us as much as for the novitiate hippie. What makes it representative and almost symbolic is its dramatic quality, and the ambiguity underlying it. The drama is their attempt to rediscover themselves as free, spontaneous and un-socialised beings. It is an attempt to get hold of the 'real' things. It is played out not only in occasional journeys to the East, but from day to day in their homeland. Although at home the drama may be as apparent, the ambiguity is more often concealed.

In Africa or the 'East' the ambiguity is never far from the surface. Those who have sat as tourists at a kerbside Moroccan café will have sensed it, as they have watched an immigrant hippie ostentatiously rejecting his homeland's pursuit of competition, prestige and status. He is a familiar figure: perfectly groomed long hair, an ornately trimmed pastel-coloured kaftan offset by decorated leather satchel, an air of effortful repose, simulating the master who has achieved some superior awareness in a culture different from his own. Yet if he has paused a moment the tourist may also have seen the fragile confidence dissolved in a moment, perhaps even by a complimentary handshake from some local village elder passing by, the Olympian detachment turned to twitching between gratitude for such acknowledgment and fear lest watching Europeans also consider it just a Western greeting for a Western European. However complete the assimilation, the hippie himself must always feel a doubt.

2

Such ambiguities may confront the observer in more dramatic form. He will see the young Arabs striving frantically for those very material possessions and comforts that the well-heeled hippie tries, equally frantically, to reject, except for a few gadgets of industrial society—like the cassette tape recorder for playing pop music—which seem to remain indispensable pillars of the hippie's detachment. The contrast and the hippie's ambivalence sum up the incongruity of people believing that they find in Morocco and the East a society that is loose and natural in some way their own is not, but without understanding the subtleties of a social order that may be as much contrived as their own, only in a different way.

In parts of Asia and Africa hippies may seek to merge with their surroundings. In their homeland, by contrast, they make themselves immediately recognisable by a combination of characteristics that seem deliberately calculated to startle. These are familiar to the conventional mind—the beads and kaftans and bare feet; the rejection of drabness and artificiality in clothing, and the use of natural colours—greens and blues and browns, and lines which express freedom and wholeness, or which cling to the wearer's body and act as a declaration of sensuality. In place of the uniforms that conventional society dons and doffs as occasion demands, they sport fantasy clothes as different and as special as can be found—old peasant hats, long dresses and shawls. They are recognisable too by the tribal dialect they have created for themselves, and which they regularly purify to keep at a distance the ever-pressing curiosity and imitation of straight society. Thus whereas in the early nineteen-sixties to be 'up-to-date' was 'swinging', and subsequently became 'with-it' and 'switched-on', by the summer of this study it had become 'together', in London at least. When they laze around now they 'loon', where previously they would 'ligg', and before that 'graze' or 'moon'. Where to be drugged in 1970 was generally to be 'spaced out' or 'turned on', before that it was generally 'hunky' or 'high'.

They are equally recognisable by their behaviour. Most important of all, in conventional eyes, is the fact that they do not work, in the sense most people understand it. They are unproductive and they are parasites. They are also 'permissive', but worse than that, they show no self-restraint, no decent respect for form and order. They are also lazy, and appear to be able to lie swooning and lost to the world for hours on end, doing nothing—which the conventional man with his compulsive commitment to action finds very odd. Then again the hippie will burst into wild activity, his whole body seemingly twitching with an excitement there is even no proper attempt to restrain.

To the 'straight' person, whether as tourist in Morocco or going about his daily business in London, the hippie is bound to appear rather odd. In the context of a particular society at a particular moment in history he may indeed be so. In a broader historical context, however, he is less strange, and certainly not unique. Many, if not all periods, have been marked by some minority who dress and act differently and who pursue their lives, by varying degrees of choice or necessity, outside that dominant social order that conditions the majority. This minority has included, in one form or another, the 'beatniks', with whom contemporary hippies have strong links. It has included also the Romantics of the early nineteenth century, and the 'bohemians' of Paris later in that century and of Bloomsbury earlier in this. Such a minority may flaunt their freedom and proclaim their indifference to social norms and values, or they may eke out a furtive and threatened existence on the farthest margins of a society, but apparent or concealed, they have usually been present.

Even their interest in societies such as Morocco and the East marks the hippies as part of a tradition. Before their name was ever heard, this century had seen the resurgence of primitive art and a persistent preoccupation with the folk tradition in music. Disturbing questions had also arisen in the minds of Europeans when they had been in their colonies long enough to reflect upon what they were doing: among writers as different as Freud and Camus, the question of what it is to be civilised became one of the deepest and most troublesome preoccupations of the Western mind, as it was forced to confront the possibilities of other ways of living than its own advanced urban industrial society, rapidly becoming as ugly as the names its social scientists coined for it. To try to understand hippies is to try to understand the contemporary embodiment of one half of this dialogue.

Hippies thus belong with the many dissident and bohemian groups which have stood aside from, and against, an increasingly complex society. Against such complexity, and its network of constraints, hippies represent an alternative vision: Elemental Man, the Noble Savage, the Natural, the Primitive. This book mainly revolves around this alternative vision. It is an exploration of various aspects of hippie cultures, but primarily it is a study of their perception of themselves and the world, of how they interpret the world through themselves, and themselves through the world, and how such interpretations guide their individual behaviour and their cultural patterns. It is an attempt to get at what is distinctive in an elusive constellation of values and behaviour, among an equally elusive constellation of people for whom 'hippies' remains the least confusing name.

A POINT OF DEPARTURE: THE EXPERIENCE OF TIME, WORK AND LEISURE

A story is told of a meeting between one of the more charismatic leaders of the London 'underground' and an old friend who was insensitive enough to ask him what work he was doing. In magisterially contemptuous tones came the reply: 'I don't work. I play.' If a single attitude was required to express the essence of hippie values this is probably the one that would be chosen, both by hippies themselves and their commentators. 'We are the secret agents of a future society free from the routine degradation of work', says the leader of the London Street Commune. 'Drop-outs are anticipating future economic policy', writes Richard Neville (1970, p. 270). 'Tomorrow you may be paid not to work—can you take it?' Our subjects' persistent concern may be the all-encompassing issue of what it means to be alive and to be civilised, but it finds its concrete embodiment here, in the meaning and value of time, work and leisure. This consequently is the area where hippies and 'straight society' most persistently conflict.

Any description of the basis of this conflict tends to become somewhat abstruse and theoretical, and thus removed from the immediate situation of the participants. Let me start then with the everyday experience of two particular people, settled in middle age, who were interviewed in pilot work for the

London Region Study. In the matter of time, work and leisure they may fitly illustrate the alternatives held before the eyes of the young.

Mr Bentley is an investment consultant. By any terms he has had a successful career. He is almost a model of what is conventionally held for imitation before the eyes of the young, not least in the way he organised his time, took his work seriously, and tried very hard at his leisure. His life is full and ostensibly rewarding, and his day carefully managed to the maximum use. In the diary he kept for us there was no hint of wasted time. The conventional time notation used in our diary form he deleted and replaced by the 24-hour clock, which epitomised that extra element of foresight and careful management by which his life was bound. As business discussion over breakfast was followed by board meeting, in its turn to give way to business discussion over lunch, little time was lost that could be put to productive purpose. Where, for Mr Bentley, was leisure found? Of conventional (and costly) diversions there were enough. But where was the magic? In what recesses of his day did the ordered mind succumb involuntarily to the disordered soul? Over what elements of his life did the writ of the unconscious extend and some element of fantasy shake the carefully contrived order of his existence.

Search as one could, diary and interview betrayed no hint of them. There were certainly moments of conventional 'leisure', but they too were measured with mechanical precision. He moved through the day like clockwork: between meetings he would wander briefly in the village streets 'to unwind', as he appropriately described it. On the journey home by train he would gaze out of the window and 'switch off'. Another Mr Bentley came through only once. At the bottom of his diary form was added a note saying that after the end of his day he had dreamed he had been sentenced to filling in two more diary sheets, and had woken up screaming. Through the satirical remark seemed to move a slight undercurrent of seriousness. To all appearances he was much too well-balanced for confronting the reality of his daily round to cause any such alarm, but the possibility should not be lost from view.

For our purpose it does not much matter if one sees as prime mover in Mr Bentley's life the commitment to work and purposive activity, 'rational' behaviour, 'achievement motivation' or whatever. What is important is the unchanging character of his perceptions and experiences, sustained through the day with an almost mechanical precision. Mr Bentley's existence was all on one plane. Wild fantasies of the unconscious did not break through. Careful advanced planning of the day had eliminated the possibilities of passion and excitement. There was no lapse into spontaneous day-dreaming or idle contemplation. To be fair, there was also no evidence that Mr Bentley was discontented with the varieties of experience his daily round allowed him. If one were to suggest to him that he was deprived, it would no doubt surprise him, in so far that anything was allowed to cause surprise. But this possibility, the hippies claimed, had to be entertained.

To see how it can be, let us turn for a moment to Mrs Adams. In passing from Mr Bentley to Mrs Adams we move from the stockbroker belt of Surrey to the buried life of Canning Town, but the locality is not important. No more is it of importance that we move also from the top class to the bottom or from wealth to relative poverty. It may just be that Mrs Adams reveals her inner life and the character of her experience more openly than Mr Bentley, or it may be that they are different. Strange and buried as she is, she somehow demonstrates that special sense of the *possible* which underpins the hippie vision. At any rate with respect to the range of her experience and sensibility the poor housewife is here the rarity, the investment consultant, Mr Bentley, commonplace. It may seem odd to use a middle-aged housewife, far removed from hippies in age and life-style, to champion their cause, but at least it may express how enduring and ubiquitous are the fundamental issues they raise.

Mrs Adams is encountered in an old semi-detached house. The wall between the two ground floor rooms has been removed to make a single long room, with bay windows at one end and french windows at the other. The atmosphere is buried and yet somehow rarefied. Flowered wallpaper, grey patterned carpeting, the usual furniture, matching as little as usual. The television is present, oddly hidden away and unobtrusive, china cabinet and bureau, aquarium and bird cage. You have all been there. Mrs Adams is tall, slim and gangling. In most ways her

life is humdrum and conventional. 'I'd like to go to clubs, but
I just don't seem to get around to it'; 'We don't seem to go
anywhere'; 'We don't do much in our leisure time but garden-
ing, knitting, washing the car down. It's a dull life, isn't it?
Dull, but secure.'

A dull and secure life, but what makes Mrs Adams different
and significant for us is that through her descriptions would at
times break a strange animation and life. Under the dreary and
strait-laced exterior she preserved an inner life of miracle
and mystery. It broke through as she spoke of those occasional
moments when inner magic transcended everyday reality, when
extremes of experience carried the sense of the self to some
special level of unity and intensity.

> If you're in a depressed state, or when you're on your
> own. If you listen to Strauss, you feel as though life is
> different, you feel as though you're a different person.
> You get a real thrill. It makes you really tingle.

> I don't really get down to the painting. If my husband's
> doing it, I just want to have a dabble. I like to look at it
> and make it real—to draw yourself away from yourself.

> I love knitting and sewing. When I've finished, I like to
> look at it and say 'I made that myself' —but it's got to be
> right. My niece wanted something knitted, so I got up at
> 7 a.m. and knitted for 10 hours. I went mad until I made
> myself sick.

From the everyday reality in which everyone is buried
Mrs Adams yearned to get away.

> Somewhere where you could say, 'Let's go, and escape'.
> To be alone, have records on full blast and go a bit mad,
> knowing you're not annoying anyone.

In a sense Mrs Adams may be slightly mad, but in this she is
probably not unusual. Within each of us, no doubt including
Mr Bentley, lies buried the fantasy of that free and spontaneous
life which the routine constraints of civilised life muffle and
mute. For most of us, most of the time, the spontaneous and
the unconscious are confined to some black night of the soul.

Mrs Adams meanwhile spent her day working at the Bank of England, checking bank notes to see that no two numbers were alike. And when after six months she found that drove her quite round the bend, she moved to machine operating, where for all its boring repetition, she could at least see the pile of work grow through the day, rather than simply watch the bank notes go their way.

Mrs Adams is important because she illustrates the possibility of other varieties of experience than the rational restraint which the ordered routines of industrial society make our primary mode of experience, and which Mr Bentley embodies. She affirms the possibility of a leisure and free time which is not a matter simply of 'unwinding' or 'switching off'; and which is also not simply consumed by commercial distractions. It is a leisure where magic, fantasy and play allow the penetration or transcendence of that armour in which our everyday selves may become encrusted. She suggests above all the possibility of some special sense of life that may come from intensified experience and which may give to the individual a deeper sense of unity and identity. If, as is certainly true, Mr Bentley is more representative of our culture than Mrs Adams, this suggests that the more intense realms of experience are being dampened and restrained. That is the hippies' fundamental belief.

Mrs Adams is not the stuff of which heroines are made, and I cannot make her seem one, but in a way she does express the hippie perception and valuation of time, work and leisure against the conventional order which Mr Bentley so fully embodies, and the two of them show the daily reality of the conflict between the hippies and the straights. What basic beliefs then underpin the common cause which Mrs Adams espouses implicitly and hippies more explicitly? The central element is a scorn of the respectable values of time and of time-keeping. This has always been a distinguishing feature of bohemian groups, but hippies carry it to an extreme. It is not just that they commit the sin of 'wasting' time. What is considered worse is that they do not take time seriously—let alone regard it as important. Perhaps the most significant gesture in the contemporary hippie Odyssey, the film *Easy Rider*, is the hero's throwing away the wrist-watch that tied him to the daily round of conventional work and conventional leisure. If it is a matter of doing their own thing, it is always *in their own time*.

They follow Ben, one of their number whom we shall shortly meet, in rejecting the time-scheduled day:

People are becoming automated. Take my father. Get up; 7.30 breakfast; out at 8; gets the 8.30 train to Charing Cross; gets on the tube, off at Oxford Circus; walks along to Hanover Square. He goes upstairs; he sits down in his office; he sits there all day; he goes out for lunch—gets himself a beer and a sandwich; comes back; carries on work; 5.30 he packs in; gets the tube back to Charing Cross—train home. I mean, what a life! Where does it get you?

The precise measurement of time and the synchronisation of behaviour is what makes possible the routinisation of work, so almost as a corollary to this rejection of time scheduling comes a rejection of the conventional pattern of work. The content of the work may be soul-destroying in itself, but to have it timed and routinised takes away the remaining opportunities of freedom and autonomy. Ben, like other hippies, has not had to look far for examples:

I had a job in an Islington factory once, standing in a factory—packing—just sticking things in—checking— signing the invoice ticket—sticking them in a big box— picking up another one—oh, my God! Physically it was very very easy, but it was a great mental strain. I found it a mental strain. There was a guy sitting next to me who'd been on it for 20 years—I tell you that sometimes I don't know how he stood it. I think he just got adjusted to it—he hadn't found a job that fitted him—he fitted himself to the job and that was that.

The hippie rejects work not only for its supposedly de-humanising content, but also for its system of organisation and what it implies for a society. A society is largely a way of organising work and distributing its product. Hippies have learnt the lesson that the social personality of man in an advanced society is largely determined by his participation in a social division of labour. This imposes what has always seemed to bohemian and beatnik groups such as hippies, to be an unacceptable degree of conformity and of restraint. Hippies acknowledge the fundamental perception of Durkheim (1933, p. 401) that without the division of labour

> Man would no longer feel about him and above him this salutary pressure of society which moderates his egoism and makes him a moral being. This is what gives moral value to the division of labour. Through it the individual becomes cognisant of his dependence upon society; from it come the forces which check and restrain him. In short, since the division of labour becomes the chief source of social solidarity, it becomes at the same time the foundation of the moral order.

To the hippie and his predecessors however, this development of a moral order, at least at the stage it reaches in an advanced industrial society, is not a matter just of the moderation of egoism, but of the repression of the instinctive life of the individual, his expressiveness and spontaneity. The conclusion of the bohemian tradition is, then, that it is only by moving outside the routines and specialisation of the world of work that the individual may preserve his natural inner 'self' and bring it to full fruition.

About this rejection of conventional notions of work there must be to the man in the street something deeply chilling. It is around work that his day is arranged and most of his life organised. By it he gains not just an economic livelihood but such social status as he has. Work constitutes a large element of his life space and conditions a large proportion of his experience. Even for the more highly educated, who have more autonomy in their work and by consequence can more control it than be controlled by it, there are equally sobering recollections: did not Marx conceive work, whatever form it took, as the fundamental condition of existence, and even Freud surely saw it as man's strongest tie to reality? There is the nagging realisation then, that there may in the hippie be represented some particularly fundamental kind of social change, not just because the culture of modern industrial society is one dominated by work, but also because most of the political and social revolutions by which its history has been punctuated have been immediately followed by entreaties that people should work harder. The hippies are different, and perhaps more dangerous to settled habits of mind.

The unkindest rub of all, however, is that having no conception of work in its conventional sense, hippies can have no conventional conception of leisure. The reason is that conventional man's concept of leisure is defined by that of work: as for Mr Bentley, it is non-work time, time 'free' from work, which is given over to relaxation after work, recuperation from its effects and diversions by which it may be put briefly out of mind. For Nick, a hippie who is our guide through much of this study, by contrast, conventional leisure is just another 'heavy game', and one where the result is rigged anyway.

> But the people who come into the pub—well I mean I talk to them, and sometimes I enjoy it. It gives me a kick sometimes—it just does. It amuses me. They come in, and you see the big smile, the big cigar hanging down, laughing at the least thing anyone says, supposedly enjoying themselves. I try to convince myself. I ask myself, are they really enjoying themselves? I mean, what's their life *to live*? You know their fun and games? It's like playing football behind a wall, on a concrete ground.

In modern bohemian thought conventional leisure is valueless also because, while it is created by a decline in work hours, it is also increasingly filled by them: working hours yield through rising productivity an increasing material output to whose consumption leisure hours are increasingly devoted. Nick therefore counts himself one of that increasing number of hippies who oppose new forms of idleness to commercial amusement.

The theoretical issue in the understanding of leisure which hippies are thus raising is how far it may be identified with 'free' time in any meaningful sense. Some philosophers, notably Marcuse, would draw a distinction between the two concepts, and say that conventional leisure is, by and large, not free. He would consider that a most pressing need for the regeneration of our culture is the transformation of commercially directed leisure into genuinely free time (1964,

p. 253). This too is a view to which most hippies would subscribe.

In the view of the hippie then, the contemporary social problem of leisure finds one form of expression in the fact that for the majority of people leisure seems largely to have ceased to be a special mode of experience, certainly special experience as Mrs Adams would understand it. Somewhere along the way it has lost for most people the scope and intensity which it seems sometimes to have had for Mrs Adams. It has become for them simply a special way of marking off and designating time in a civilisation where the compartmentalisation and allocation of time is a consideration of pressing importance. When we speak of leisure we have generally in mind 'leisure time', the part of each day which is free from work and the more obvious commitments and constraints of living. Leisure is just leisure time, and how it is filled or experienced is of less moment. Of those who do not conceive leisure in primarily temporal terms, most apparently conceive it in terms of what is, with time, the other chief preoccupation of the Western mind: activity. Leisure is then identified exclusively with a specific range of activities, primarily sporting and social pastimes. Within what segment of time they are performed is less important; only the nature of the activity is important. They have in common with the clock watchers, however, the fact that they place little emphasis on the quality of experience and state of mind of the participant.[2]

True to their dismal science economists, moreover, now begin to tell us that the rising productivity and increasing affluence which mark our age are more likely to constrain and limit free time than expand it.

> The scope of idleness depends upon the level of income. If incomes are low there can be long periods of enforced idleness or passivity. Individuals will then have at their disposal economic free time in the true sense. They are waiting for Godot. At a higher level of income we find voluntarily chosen idleness, which is reflected in people taking life easy and finding this enjoyable. The pace of life is not rapid. But as incomes continue to rise, the demands for yield on the use of time increase. As a result fewer and

fewer 'slacks' will be tolerated. The degree to which time is actively utilised will increase. The pace of life will quicken. (Linder, 1970, p. 16.)

The more goods that are produced, the more our time is absorbed in consumption and indeed in the mere management and servicing of the goods themselves. Linder's analysis suggests a picture of consumption as compulsion, which is the very opposite of leisure and autonomy.

Like many others, hippies would argue then, that conventional leisure is not the antithesis of the alienated world of work but, with its pressures, identifies itelf completely with that world. At any rate the requirements of the consumer industry, which of course have to be understood in terms of the economic law of rational production, do their best, while providing him with a certain 'freedom of choice', to deprive the individual of the freedom *not to choose*. In this way the conformity of modern productive society extends to the consumer as well. The pressures on him as consumer are hardly less than those on him as producer.

Increased leisure time becomes nothing more than increased compulsion to consume and to produce consumer goods— and a profit-conscious consumer industry is glad to apply itself to these alienated requirements. The leisure industry, offering cheap amusement, distraction, sport, games, ready-made culture and the consumer goods of the sub-culture, threatens to destroy people's exertions and decision-making spontaneity and self-determination. (Heitger, 1970, pp. 55–6.)

To hippies today, as to their predecessors in other generations, it seems that the everyday lives of young people are largely constrained within a single mode of experience which is time-bound, routinised and lacking in autonomy and creativity, and thus set firmly in the conventional category of 'work', as against true leisure. The real values of the hippie—play, spontaneity and fantasy—and the further excesses of passion or contemplation can consequently find little expression.

For such a condition, so far as it exists, it would be easy to blame the cultural apparatus itself, and in this way locate the problem outside the individual, but hippies have absorbed the lessons of a psychoanalytic tradition which reminds us that this may be wrong. Consciously or unconsciously, people may connive at their own enslavement. If people's daily experience is limited and constrained, it may be because they themselves wish to avoid the alternative. Bohemian groups have always believed something of the sort. With regard to particular contemporary problems of leisure, for example, Alexander Reid Martin speaks of a 'self-alienation' which man has used as a crutch or protection through the ages and to which he now resorts as he confronts the possibilities of leisure and free time. Martin's definition (1961, pp. 156–65) of self-alienation comes close to the diagnosis that most hippies would give of contemporary society: an unconscious dissociative process involving denial of, or escape from, those inner conflicting feelings, wishes and impulses which are expressions of the true self. It is a negation, a repression of genuine spontaneous feelings, thoughts and actions. He distinguishes five patterns of self-alienation whose symptom is the 'loss of leisure'. They closely mirror the intellectual position I have outlined.

In one of these patterns, the 'conditional pattern', Martin suggests that while work and leisure should naturally complement each other in a healthy growth process, a mode of self-alienation may lead people to operate exclusively on a 'debit–credit, reward and punishment system, where work becomes the payment, penalty or punishment for leisure and, on the other hand, leisure becomes the reward for work. *All* their play, leisure, relaxation are thus exclusively conditional and felt to be only rightfully forthcoming on condition that they pay for it, with labour and sweat.' He distinguishes another compulsive pattern where the individual retreats all the time to reactions that have a 'must' or imperative quality about them. 'We can appreciate the difference between the man who *must* play golf and the man who *wants* to play golf. Between the man who *must* win at all times to the man who *wants* to win.' As another form of self-alienation and loss of leisure he distinguishes that fear of the unconscious which shows itself in the avoidance of 'free association': 'Free association is in every respect and in essence a leisure process. Compulsive control, which prevents this natural leisure process from asserting itself, stems from fear of the unconscious.' The two final patterns are, however, the most significant for us. One is the 'Super-intellectual Pattern' (1961, pp. 161–2):

> Compulsive use of the intellect to repress the sensual and emotional is familiar to us all; we have, however, failed to note how much of this pattern is characterised by great glorification of the mind at work and complete contempt and rejection of the mind at play. These individuals convince themselves that solely through intellectual work, intensive thinking through, logical reasoning and figuring out can they reach solutions and find answers.
>
> It was perhaps the glorification of this compulsive thinking that St Paul in the Fourth Chapter of Ephesians called the 'vanity of the mind' which we are told in the King James version of the Bible accompanies 'blindness of the heart' and leads to 'alienation' from life and 'being past feeling'.

Finally, the 'frictionless pattern', which consists in the avoidance of excitement, passion and conflict.

> The frictionless pattern tends to make leisure less and less possible. With each avoidance of healthy interplay, sport and conflict, the individual feels increasingly weaker and this leads to alienation from others. Similarly in his inner life he avoids his inner conflicts by alienation, as it were from himself . . . The healthy friction of formative interplay and conflict in the outer and inner world provides the 'spark of life' and the warmth and fire of our emotional being.

Such a diagnosis of contemporary society could be elaborated in many different ways. My purpose in outlining it is not to reach any sort of conclusion on its validity, but rather to illustrate the general area of values and attitudes in which the conflicts between hippie and straight society are conventionally located. Every aspect of such a diagnosis has a long history. I shall not suggest that hippies are familiar with it in any detail, nor that they consciously draw upon it. They generally do not. Nevertheless the issues which they raise, and the particular language in which they discuss them, are drawn, in part at least, from this reservoir of doubt and alternative belief, which has been present almost as long as industrial society itself. I shall argue throughout this study that the behaviour and values of hippies are guided primarily by particular configurations of individual and personal experiences. But the fact that their dissent may be expressed at all, either in individual thought or joint social action, is owed in part at least to the presence of this language and framework of ideas.

THE WORLD THEY HAVE LEFT

These observations may in due course help locate my subjects philosophically. How are they to be located in social terms? How far, for example, are they representative of their generation? Are they the articulators and spokesmen of a discontent felt by the rest? Or are they just very odd and rare? How far indeed do they and their generation subscribe to the values and behaviour of their elders? Such questions have obvious importance. Like any other identifiable kind of people, my subjects arose in a particular social context, and continued to be conditioned by it. The very fact that they tried so hard to escape and undo the effects of the socialisation processes of childhood may in a way indicate how strongly they felt their influence.

Such questions are usually raised and usually answered in terms of a 'generation gap' which is presumed to have existed for some years. The young, or most of them, it is said, are in important ways different from what their parents' generation are or ever were—not least in their attitudes to time, work and leisure. According to this account, the young as a whole are different and hippies only an extreme example of such difference. This account is so persistent because, at its core, it is platitudinous. The divisions produced by historical and inter-generational change are always important, but also easily exaggerated. With regard to the concerns of this book, we shall in fact see that the more important divisions are enduring ones, running through generations rather than between them.

Nevertheless it is important to bear in mind what is special about the whole generation of which the protagonists of this book are part; those people who in 1970 were between the ages of seventeen and twenty-five. In so far as it is about a part of this generation it is about the particular events they have experienced.[3] A few particular and disjointed examples may suggest the contours of the time and the people, and the readers' reflection can fill them out. Although too young to remember post-war privation and scarcity, let alone the war itself, they are just old enough to have experienced the brief elation and excitement of the CND crusades. Unable to conceive a time when the atomic bomb did not exist, they find it difficult to think of it as a rectifiable mistake of policy rather than as a perpetually possible tomorrow. Their perception is dominated less by the classical elegances of science than by the ambiguities and paradoxes of a rampant technology—from its belittlement in Vietnam to its triumphs in space. More immediately they are perhaps the first generation not to recall life without television and the last to recall coal fires. Most important of all, beat music reached them before they were too old to respond to it, and drugs became accessible to them when their identities were not yet so irrevocably defined as not to reward further exploration. This generation is thus unique and special, as everyone before it has been.

Nevertheless the balance of opinion among those who examine the matter at all deeply, seems to be that there are not those broad and dramatic differences from the previous generation that the popular conception of a generation gap implies. What research usually shows is rather, for the large majority, the remarkable continuity of behaviour from one generation to another.[4] The study by Butler and Stokes was a timely reminder that parents' political affiliation was still the best predictor of the political attachment of youth (Butler and Stokes, 1969). Other studies of specific factors also suggest that 'almost any restraint that parents implant in their sons and daughters hangs on, affecting their behaviour' (Lubell, 1968). Perhaps the most dramatic evidence comes from Lubell's research on what is reputedly the group for whom the gap is most extreme, American college students. His study reveals that only about one in ten American students show drastic changes from their parents, that one-third show no important differences from their parents and that another one-third only moderate changes. While in the extreme group personal behaviour does differ markedly—particularly drug use and sexual relations—more than half would still give their children much the same up-bringing as they had. Lubell's conclusion is that parents have not been rendered obsolete but continue to exert an almost ineradicable influence on their children. If this is true overall, how far does it hold for what will be the recurring concerns of the people in this book: time and routine, work and leisure, freedom and play.

We find, first of all, that in the matter of their satisfaction with paid routine employment, the broad majority of young people are as different from the hippies as are the majority of the older generation. The general sample of 212 young people aged seventeen to twenty-four in the London Region Study were asked directly how satisfied they were with their work. Of the total only 12 per cent replied explicitly that they were not satisfied, the remainder indicating that they were either very (45 per cent) or fairly (43 per cent) satisfied. Yet very many more than one in eight must be engaged in work which seems from the outside to be humdrum and routine. They seemed even less discontented with their leisure time experience, or so another result implied: while a large majority (8 per cent) were very or fairly satisfied with their work, a majority (67 per cent) also claimed to gain more satisfaction from their leisure than from their work.

It is perhaps not surprising that the broad majority of young people should express little discontent with their leisure. Young people are in many ways a privileged class, at least when this is measured by indices such as available free time and disposable income. By and large they work shorter hours than their elders, and, at least until family commitments alter matters, they have relatively high disposable incomes. Whereas 72 per cent of those aged twenty to twenty-four were working 45 hours a week or less, by the mid-forties this proportion has fallen to 56 per cent. Whereas only 9 per cent of them are working very long hours—more than 55 per week—the proportion has risen to 21 per cent for those in their thirties.

A generally similar pattern prevails with income. The young manual worker may quickly come near to parity with his older and more experienced counterpart. One of the more notable economic trends of recent years has been the relative increase in the prosperity of the young. Using 1947 as the base—100, the index of hourly earnings of manual workers for the British girl in 1968 was 404 and for the boy was 472. By contrast, the figure from the same base was 350 for a working woman and 361 for a working man. (Department of Employment, *British Labour Statistics,* pp. 110–19.)

Young people today come nearer than almost all other sections of the community to constituting a leisure class. If anything the figures for working hours and income understate this. A better indicator of their privileged position is the extent to which they participate in (and often dominate) the round of sports and social pastimes which are outside the necessary cycle of daily living and have most fully the character of play, socialising and escapism. By this criterion youth seems particularly privileged. In the London Region Study the average number of different sporting and social activities that the individual had taken part in at least once in the previous year fell steadily from nineteen for those aged eighteen or nineteen to nine for those aged sixty-five to sixty-nine. If only those done more frequently are included the result is similar. The average number that each person did at least twelve times a year fell over the same age-range from eleven to six.

If it is against the work ethic society that the young people described in this study are in revolt, they necessarily find themselves in opposition to the majority of their own generation as well as to generations older than their own. On the surface at least, there is little to suggest that the majority of young people are seriously discontented with their work and leisure lives, and indeed little reason why they should be. Relatively at least, they seem privileged. This is not to say that the often repeated indictments of conventional conceptions of time, work and leisure that I have described are invalid. All it suggests is that, whether valid or not, most young people are either unaware of them or, if aware, are not caused any serious concern or dissatisfaction by them.

It is with work rather than leisure that the absence of discontent is most surprising, but such absence may only imply that for most young people the supposedly traditional values of the work ethic society are still important. The evidence certainly suggests this. Such a possibility should cause no surprise to followers of the leading contemporary writers on leisure, who have more and more cast doubt on the liberating potential of increased leisure time. Riesman turned from an early optimism about the value and significance of leisure to a later belief that it was not an area whose particular satisfactions could compensate or substitute for the deprivations of the world of work.[5] It is to this later conclusion rather than to the earlier one that the London Region Survey lent some tentative support. The same young people who for the most part expressed contentment with their work and leisure were asked how far they agreed with three statements designed to show whether the traditional protestant ethic evaluation of leisure—as a dependent and rather guilt-ridden appendage of work—still prevailed. None of the results suggest that leisure is perceived or experienced as an area of autonomy and creativity.

The first statement—'One should not only work hard, one should play hard'—was designed to give some clue as to how far the respondents identified leisure as an area of lightness, freedom and spontaneity, existing in its own right, and outside the heaviness and seriousness of work. Even allowing for the fact that the final phraseology of the question to some extent led the respondents, the result tends to the conclusion that for a large proportion leisure is almost as much part of the realm of rational and purposeful deliberateness as is work itself: 65 per cent of the sample endorsed the proposition, 30 per cent of them strongly. Play is traditionally—and almost by definition—the area of spontaneity and lightness, of activity undertaken for meanings within itself rather than outside it. The expression 'play hard' immediately brings in an element of purposeful intensity and achievement motivation quite negating the original concept. There is a sense in which to 'play hard' is to work. If this result can be relied upon, for a majority of young people, leisure, despite its scope and quantity, remains partly lodged under the shadow of a work ethic which must largely deprive it of real integrity and autonomy. Since the one thing on which all hippie and 'underground' writers agree is a commitment to the concept of play, the schism between themselves and the conventional young people is here particularly apparent.

The second statement—'leisure must be earned to be enjoyed'—represents the core value of the work society, the moral ascendancy of work. Here again there was a majority willing to endorse the statement—59 per cent. It cannot be said for certain that agreement was based on some deep-rooted sense of guilt about pleasure that had not been paid for, rather than representing some pragmatic belief that work and leisure enriched each other by contrast and alternation. Nevertheless the fact that the verb was in imperative mood—that leisure *must* be earned to be enjoyed—suggests moral evaluation rather than pragmatic reflection upon experience. Reactions to the final statement—'leisure must be constructive to be satisfying'—certainly do little to dispel this conclusion. The result here must be taken with particular caution: there is of course a range of interpretations that could be placed upon the word 'constructive'. It was nevertheless used because it most fully evokes the purposive and utilitarian orientation to leisure: a belief that leisure is not an end-in-itself but subordinate to some end product. It comes nearest to expressing the belief that leisure should be work. We found that 45 per cent of the total sample in fact endorsed the statement.

Such results are difficult to interpret. Because no one can say with any confidence how prevalent the work ethic has been in the past, at least among the broad mass of working people rather than among particular sects or entrepreneurial groups, one does not know where to place the emphasis. The only firm conclusion is that, in so far as the moral and philosophical position of hippies rejects conventional routines of work and leisure and places emphasis on play and spontaneity, it finds little reflection in the attitudes and values of the broad mass of young people.

It is not only in their attitudes to work and leisure that the majority of young people show themselves relatively contented and far removed from the position adopted by the people we shall see in this study. The broad pattern of their aims, into which these attitudes are meshed, shows little sign of radical change from long-established social values. If what are usually presumed to be the settled goals and values of our social order—the nuclear family, the steady job or career, power and responsibility—are under assault, it is certainly not from most young people. This is suggested by a question in which respondents in the general sample were asked to rate as

very important, fairly important or not important, each of a
series of six possible aims in life:

1 To have a secure and settled family life.
2 To make a success of one particular job or career.
3 To keep on having new experiences and trying new things.
4 To have a lot of free time to spend as you want.
5 To have a creative job that allows you to develop your
   abilities.
6 To have a good deal of power and responsibility.

It would be wrong to draw precise conclusions from such an
encompassing question: all the aims may be in some way
'important', and on the responses to separate statements no
great emphasis should be laid. The primary aim of the question
was to see what respondents opted for within two different
ranges of alternatives. How far, first, would evidence bear out
the suggestion that young people generally are, like hippies,
more concerned with having a wide range of experience rather
than with achieving success within one particular kind of work?
And which ranks as most important among the various kinds
of freedom—'free time', or the freedom provided by a creative
job, or that provided by power and responsibility? To the
first question the answer is tentative and ambiguous: while
32 per cent gave them equal rating, 35 per cent evaluated success
at one career as more important than a continually widening
range of experience, and 33 per cent reversed the order. The
young person would risk the particular sin of dullness who did
not rate 'new experience' as important, so it is perhaps a little
surprising that more respondents rated success in one career
higher than new experience than did the reverse. The pattern
of preference between the various dimensions of freedom is
more clear-cut: while 34 per cent ranked 'a creative job that
allows you to develop your abilities' highest, a further 50 per
cent ranked it equally highest with one or both of the others.
Well over twice as many respondents rated it clearly highest
than did free time.

Such evidence makes it difficult to consider hippies as one
extreme end of a spectrum along which all young people can be
located, explicable in fundamentally similar terms as the rest.
I shall therefore take the fact of their difference as my preli-

minary assumption, and see how far they may be explained in their own right and on their own terms. As the reader moves through this study he should bear in mind that hippies are in fundamental ways quite untypical of their generation. They are what they seem, a world away from the placid contentment of the unrebellious majority by whom they are on all sides surrounded.

Sympathy and misunderstanding

Hippies cannot, however, be entirely 'a tribe of their own', to use the words of one general sample respondent. They may not be *of* the dominant culture, but they are within it, so there are some links and common themes that draw the two together. Even among the conforming majority, there were small but potentially important groups who echoed some of their attitudes and values. Some 23 per cent, for example, particularly heavily represented among the more educated, saw their own generation as less acquisitive than their parents', and steadily turning from that commitment to affluence and material prosperity they often felt had too fully absorbed their parents. Others claimed, generally with approval, that there was more tolerance (31 per cent) and less hypocrisy (41 per cent) among the young.

These, however, were only straws in the wind, and rather insubstantial ones at that; they reinforced my initial assumption rather than detracted from it. Far more substantial was the evidence that emerged of mutual mistrust, and more important, of mutual incomprehension between straight majority and hippie minority. No precise measure of this was possible, but some general indication is given by responses to one particular question. Those interviewed in the general sample were asked what they thought was meant by the ubiquitous slogan of hip culture, 'to do your own thing in your own time', the prescription which is the hippies' answer to the routine labour of the work ethic society, and how far they themselves were in sympathy with it as they defined it. The purpose was to discover what proportion of the sample would reveal by implication a knowledge and understanding of the people with whom these values are most associated.

Among hippies there is of course no undisputed definition,

but for the person who moves among them its meaning is reasonably clear, if not easily expressed. Let us say for the moment that it means to find identity and fulfilment through some activity, or more broadly, some way of life, which to the particular individual is spontaneously absorbing. The key elements are identity, spontaneity and autonomy. How many gave definitions which involved some combination of these elements, and with which the subjects of this study would concur? The answers were inevitably diffuse and difficult to allocate but only about 6 per cent of replies seemed interpretable in this way. The number who *might* know was in any event much less important than the number who certainly did not know, and for a large proportion it was clear that the slogan held no identifiable or articulable meaning at all; or if it had a meaning it was one remote from their own experience and to which they were not privy and at which they could hardly even guess. Within this category fell nearly one-third of the general sample of young people:

Good grief. I've never heard that one before.

Haven't a clue. Hippies are a degrading part of our generation. I can't understand them and I've no time for them at all.

I've no idea. I've never heard of this. Hippies are a tribe of their own—they don't mix with us, we don't mix with them. As long as they stay away from us it's perfectly all right.

One-third of the young people interviewed thus felt so remote from the hippie world that they could not even guess at what such a strange notion might involve. Another 7 per cent got it completely wrong: they went to the opposite extreme, and identified it with behaving in accordance with some external moral compulsion or prescript. The remainder divided between those (35 per cent) who just conceived of it as something from which one got pleasure and enjoyment; and those (20 per cent) who came nearest to the people in this study and who felt that it meant to act in some sense 'naturally', according to their own natures or some inner dynamic.

There was, therefore, certainly ignorance. Sometimes, however, there was also sympathy. Although 21 per cent expressed explicit disagreement with the injunction to 'do your own thing', there was often among them as much as among the remainder who would express no explicit disagreement with it, a certain underlying sympathy, whatever doubts they might be prey to.

I suppose I basically disagree but I can see some merits in it. People should do what they enjoy.

They do what they want to do—freedom. I've got nothing against hippies in the first place. I've got a small amount of jealousy of them. I'd like to measure myself up against them but I've got too many responsibilities—debts to repay.

To live life as you want to live it and not be sort of bullied into things simply because it's the right thing to do. I think you can agree with what hippies are doing and feeling without being what they are. Everyone's got something against boring routine for the rest of their lives.

Among some young people there is then a measure of sympathy and even envy of hippies, a sort of longing to believe, even though it is only a qualification on a dominant attitude of mistrust and incomprehension. Straight majority and hip minority start and remain worlds apart.

THE SAMPLE AND RESEARCH METHODS

I have so far identified the people who are the subject of this study mainly by the more obvious ways in which they differ from the broad mass of young people. For the most part, I shall leave it there, and not try to 'locate' them in any more specific manner. That would have demanded different methods and procedures than those I have followed, and would in any case have taken me away from my central concern with the particular character of the hippie's experience and perceptions and the patterns into which he assembles them. The aims of this study meant that the research was bound to give more attention to entering the deep and private areas of an individual's experience than to worrying whether the 'sample' was itself precisely representative of any given population. Some words on this latter point are, however, necessary, even though they do not carry complete conviction, even with the writer.

The statistics quoted in the previous section were based on interviews conducted with a standardised questionnaire with 212 respondents aged seventeen to twenty-four in a random electoral register sample of the London Metropolitan Region. They may be generalised with some confidence to the population of that age-range in the region, and, with more qualifications, beyond it.[6] No such recognised procedures were available for selecting the hippies who will be contrasted with them. There was no register of hippies, heads and freaks. Indeed hardly any, among themselves at least, would agree on how they were to be defined and recognised. The researcher could do only two things. One was to proceed by hunch and impression, and go where common repute had it that the kinds of people in whom he was interested were to be found. The other was to avoid categories so far as possible, and instead concentrate upon describable individuals for whom labels were unnecessary or inadequate.

Most of the material on which this study is based was gathered by observation and by tape-recorded interviews and discussions. To some extent also I 'participated', as the researcher in such a setting is bound to do. Unlike some researchers, however, I made no attempt to assume the appearance and habits of the people whose lives I was investigating. This was a deliberate choice: the researcher can never do that fully and effectively, and it may seem deceitful to try. If he expects his informants to be honest with him, he must be honest with them. The quotations included in the study are verbatim. The longer ones have been edited to exclude material which is repetitious and irrelevant, but I have done this sparingly. These were the chosen procedures.

I then went to two areas which seemed—in 1970 at least—obvious resorts of the kind of people in whom I was interested. In each case I was initially introduced and guided by someone who knew the area better than I did. I then proceeded by chain-interviewing to get to know as many people as I could. Although in a casual and unstructured way I talked to hundreds, I was more concerned to get to know a few in depth. For the most part this study is based only on some thirty people, drawn about evenly from the two groups.

Who were these groups, and what was there in common within the groups and between them? The first was a network of hippies living in the Ladbroke Grove area of West London: to define them as hippies might not in their own mind be entirely exact, but they were at least a group who were bohemian in their explicit rejection of the dominant society and its ways and in their articulated pursuit of a different style of life; and 'hippie' to the extent that this was as nearly as one could categorise the style of their bohemianism. The second was part of the sub-culture of West End hippies, young 'social derelicts', in current terminology, who frequented the inner city centred predominantly on Piccadilly, and who shared much of the life-style, attitudes and behaviour of those around Ladbroke Grove. The two groups had much in common besides their youth and their status as outsiders, whether 'dropped-out' or 'pushed-out'. They shared, as we shall see, the values of hippie culture, its emphasis on physical euphoria and sexual enjoyment, its emphasis on immediate satisfaction rather than the deferral of gratification, its belief in spontaneity and expressivity, in 'doing your own thing' rather than becoming enmeshed in bureaucratic procedures. They shared also the attachments that accompany such values, above all to pop music and drugs. There were of course in their life-style also important differences between the two, which derived in particular from the fact that the latter sub-culture was far more influenced than the former by the prevalence of hard drugs.

Within and between the two groups there were obvious differences which will become clear, of age, sex, nationality, family and educational history, besides others. At this point I need refer to only a few. While exact measures of the difference cannot be given, it was clear that the West End hippies were by and large less well-educated, of lower social class of origin, and somewhat younger than the networks around Ladbroke Grove. They also showed more obviously the effects of mental disturbance or some disaster in their personal histories. These differences combined to make the groups fit rather different categories in the sociology of deviance. Although overall I did not find this a useful perspective for analysing the two groups, it can illuminate some aspects of their behaviour. In Merton's terms the West End hippies might be characterised as retreatists, in so far as they rejected both the cultural goals and the institutionalised means of society (1938, 1957). The Ladbroke Grove hippies might, by contrast, be more readily characterised as rebels in that they not only rejected the goals and means of society but also substituted new ones. Whereas this latter group could create its own life-style—if one may use again that so much abused term—the former could only attack what existed.

What this comes to is that the two groups were at extreme ends of the spectrum of hip-culture: while the hippies of Ladbroke Grove could number themselves to some extent among its leaders and initiators, those of the West End were among the weakest and least discerning of its followers and imitators. In so far as these two ends of the spectrum were covered, so too were the possibilities between them: collectively at least, the people described in this study were in some degree representative of 'hippies', even if not in any rigorous sense.

In place of the two I have included, I could obviously have chosen any number of other groups, concerned with any number of different things. It may be argued that I should have included also groups based on communes, arts labs, street theatre troupes or any number of others. That I did not reflects both limitation of resources and an early conclusion that such semi-formal groupings change so rapidly in form and membership that they do not provide an appropriate framework and focus for this kind of research. I have covered, I think, the two most critical sub-populations in my chosen universe, and believe this sufficient for the kind of interpretation with which I am concerned.

When I said that there were within these two groups important variations by the main social and demographic variables, I was paying no more than lip-service to a professional tradition. In this study they will in fact be largely ignored: I started with a concern for them but soon came to reject them as of little explanatory power. Not only have I given scant attention to the sort of information which usually seems important: the reader will see that this study has also not followed properly the usual formula of sociological investigation, that situations create attitudes which in turn determine behaviour. This too did not seem to me to fit very well. This book mainly relies instead on the description and explanation of that common structure of meaning which hippies impose upon the world. I believe this meaning derives from experiences and feelings which are largely independent of the social structure itself. The study thus tries to show how feelings, intuitions and experiences interact to form that vision of oneself and the world from which individual behaviour and social circumstances derive.

The structure and content of this book reflect this. The next section is a description, mainly in the hippies' own words, of their world: like the different worlds each of us inhabits, most of it is in their minds. Having described this, in the following chapter I try to analyse how it is created, illustrating the process from the experience of several young people who had quite recently joined it. In a subsequent chapter I describe the way it is sustained, mainly by the entrepreneurs of drugs and underground music, and the social services and private sacraments they provide. I also try to analyse a little more clearly the structure of meaning that ties together the various elements of this world, and question finally how far it amounts to a viable foundation for a way of life.

II

THE LIFE OF THE LONDON HIPPIE

SCENE W.II

Initiation

Our arrival that first afternoon at Carraghbay Terrace was unannounced, but not unexpected. We were directed to what had once been the basement flat. It had now resumed the dark and secretive character of a basement, while discarding all the clutter, trappings and vain embellishments that reflect the presence of a living, if uncaring, occupant. 198 Carraghbay Terrace was between tenants. Formally it was still rented by Sophie Driberg, except that she and her household had moved to another flat, and it had thus been left to the mercies of her children. The flat was for a period rejected and excluded, outside the ebb and flow of everyday life by which all the other buildings in the street were beaten from moment to moment. It may then have been a particularly appropriate locale for the ritual ceremonies by which Sophie's children, Jason and Helen, and their outsider friends celebrated their detachment from the everyday world.

On arrival the outer door was found barred to entrance except by some magical combination of knocks which neither we nor even our guides knew. An interminable time seemed to ensue while attempts were made to arouse attention and negotiate admission without causing such alarm and commotion that the activities within would be brought to a prompt and frantic conclusion.

We walked at last down a dark corridor which had begun to acquire a smell of fetid damp and insettling marihuana. The final door presented much less of an obstacle. The inevitable questions were hesitant, apologetic, and useless, presenting no possible threat to anyone bent on deception. It was, we came to realise, part of the ritual. We were the outsiders now, and the dynamics of exclusion were practised upon us: the just visible suppression of doubt, the curious looks, the contrived gestures of accommodation.

Our eyes floated around the room gradually growing accustomed to the darkness and the sting of incense. We noticed the young girl who moved discreetly about the room, allaying fears at our abrupt arrival and throwing comforting glances upon us. We noticed another whose incongruously chic clothes showed the never far-distant influence of the on-ground world. She appeared the parvenu, but did not seem to feel it, as she skipped about the room with an almost animal delight. We noticed the short, plump girl, no trace of make-up, raven-black fuzzy hair, conventional kaftan and beads, who sat cross-legged, utterly absorbed in—of all things—knitting, which she seemed to do by movement not just of her arms but of her whole body, in perfect rhythm. All the men appeared, to the untutored eye, to be swooning, except for the one to whose lot it fell to summon up energy enough for the time-consuming and not uncomplicated procedures of rolling the joint.

In the corner of the room, so set that the whole room seemed wrapped around it, stood a set of drums, beautiful and costly. Behind them, fondling them, dismissing them, assaulting them, sat the young host, dark, slim, his limpid expressionless face a *tabula rasa* on which the world was forbidden to write. When every few minutes he broke off playing, he spoke to no one, and only the occasional whisperings in his ear by the young girl undermined the impression of a dumb mute, to whom language had long ceased to convey anything worth expressing or receiving.

We were by now seated on cushions upon the floor. There began endless solicitations about our comfort: the spare cushions were offered not one but a dozen times. The solicitations were expressed with an immediate and disconcerting earnestness. They went beyond the civility or even kindness that a first-met stranger might expect, and up-turned all those careful gradations of behaviour that reflected and defined relationships of different degrees of intimacy. If such overweening concern was available for the stranger, what was reserved for the friend? We felt morally chastened: perhaps our doubts about their sincerity only confirmed how far we ourselves must already be among the lost.

Jason was not impervious to our presence, for all his silence and apparent unconcern. What was a performance before our arrival was now an exhibition. The same staccato climax was played, again and again, each time louder and faster: each time more exhaustingly. The swooning men would come briefly alive, and sit, lotus-like, beating out the rhythm on their thighs or improvising instruments from shells, spoons, or the few such implements as littered the floor. The music was searing, a perpetual catharsis which, like the occasion itself, had no beginning, no end, no purpose or pattern. Whether it was all that the instrument allowed, or all that the drummer knew, seemed irrelevant.

We sat there in the darkness, naively expecting something to happen. Why else would they have come: it certainly was not to talk. Nor was it to smoke pot, something done so endlessly and so casually in their own flats, in their twos and threes, as not to merit a special gathering of ten or twelve. The joint was passed around the circle with ritual care, but no one paid much attention to its progress. Perhaps they had come to see Jason's performance? But even that aroused only desultory attention. The occasion was like a performance of Steppenwolf's Pablo, but it was not only or mainly that. The real reason gradually became apparent. On the floorboards in front of the old brick fireplace, now exciting the animated attention of the girls stood a fine old Chinese blue teapot, exquisitely shaped, a work of beauty and craftsmanship. Beside it was a single, equally exquisite, handleless tea-cup. There could be no doubt about it: they had come to tea. That it was in part to escape from the city, sunshine and civilisation above and around this dark, humid basement, was irrelevant. The play was the thing. The tea was heated and brewed and delicately poured. The single cup was passed from hand to mouth to hand around the circle, not to be drunk but merely sipped. It was an act of communion, to be performed with a sensuous delicacy. Except for an occasional few bars, the drums were now largely silent. Such conversation as there had ever been was now largely ended. The cup was passed back to be refilled several times.

The occasion, trivial as it seemed to the outsider, at last found a form, a sense of development and drama.

Soon after the other visitors began, one by one, to depart without words or thanks or ceremony. We ourselves stumbled awkwardly out, to be caught by surprise by the sun, the dust and the noise—not surprising in themselves, only as the symbols of a mid-afternoon when the world was waiting. If it had been late at night it would somehow all have seemed much more proper.

Styles of commitment: Elaine and Annette   Unmistakably it was Jason who sat behind the drums, and the small lithe girl who every few minutes would go and whisper in his ear his sister, Helen. They were the children of Sophie by her second or third husband and all three now lived from an allowance made available by the father's family. Sophie was American by nationality, but that had never meant much. They had moved just recently from Paris, in the wake of the difficult times that followed the 1968 troubles. Helen had now settled into an expensive school, and somewhat to the surprise of her mother, was intent upon becoming a doctor. She smoked pot with the rest, and engaged in all the other casual observances of the hip world. What she disliked about it was its instability and disorder, and particularly their persistent moves from one flat to another. Jason, aged only eighteen, was neither at school nor at work, and indeed had done neither since he was sixteen.

'You know, hippie society is exactly like society itself.' The speaker was Elaine, the smartly-dressed girl, who had been jumping around wildly in the basement in obvious delight at the whole experience.

You have the people who are very rich and who don't know what to do in life. And they think the best thing to do is to go around dressed in fantastic clothes. Which is the equivalent of the *incroyable merveilleuse* during the French Revolution. They want really to show off because they don't know what to do with their money any longer.

Then you have another type of hippie which is people who don't really need to work in life, like Sophie, for example, and who don't want to lead the boring life of a bourgeois. These people are pretending they are hippies. And then you have the revolutionary people, the anarchists, who cannot really fit in society, so the only place to be is with a movement.

Then you have the real hippie, the one who is enlightened, who really believes in the philosophy, who really lives their ideals. They really think that we are at one with the whole universe, and that we shouldn't be interested in the material side of life. That we are spirit carried around in a body.

Elaine herself was now spending all her time with the small hippie community, the core of which had been present in the basement. How did she fit into the constellation whose limits she had defined? She clearly did not feel one of them and liked to keep a certain detachment from them. Like many others she lived among them for particular reasons of her own. But what separated her from the others became quickly apparent.

I hate the very idea of sitting in a room doing nothing— unless you are stoned. If you are not stoned, I don't see the point. It might be due to my nature: restless: a very nervous person. If hippies are sitting in a place doing nothing it is either because they are tripping or they are stoned.

They pretend: every single hippie has a guitar. But who is really playing it? It's a cover, an illusion.

I think this would be the case of Jason. He keeps on saying he can do anything in life. What can he really do?

Elaine seemed to think their lives were empty, but continued to live with them. They seemed to her somehow to embody the life and magic she had been denied in her teenage. That had been strict, conventional and repressed: and her sense of herself had suffered as a consequence. She was here trying to discover the *real* person a real teenage might have produced. She had experienced a transformation of a sort and it was this that had led her to come to London from her native France.

I used to feel separated from other people. But since I've been in London, it's all gone. It was very good for me to come over here. When I first went to university, I was

35

extremely mixed up. And I didn't have any teenage. And all the friends I had had all had a pretty good time. They went out to clubs, and dancing, and they knew a lot about music. And I didn't know anything about all those things. It was at the time of the Beatlemania, you know? And I became a Beatle fan, and I started to have fun, and it made things worse at home, because when I would go back home my parents couldn't understand why I was enjoying myself.

Elaine's commitment was then for a particular purpose. She refused to acknowledge that total commitment to her present way of life that all the others felt, and in this she was particularly unlike Annette, who for several years now had been stumbling around the hippie centres of Europe, Asia and North Africa and had totally identified herself with its ways. Annette had also been at Carraghbay Terrace that afternoon. In most ways Elaine and Annette were as extreme a contrast as this sub-culture produced. In other ways they were alike, and like many of their friends. Both came from relatively strict and religious backgrounds, had been accustomed to a certain measure of restricting comfort, and had been given what they now felt to have been the doubtful advantages of a good, but even more restricting, education.

What else did they share? Drugs and music, of course, but beliefs and attitudes too, a preoccupation with time and reality, and particularly the complex relation between them, a rejection of the 'heavy games' that pass in straight society for 'meaningful relationships', a concern with the occult, with animistic creeds and with the East.

There is no reality [Elaine would remark]. There is just a fantastic atomic explosion. We are millions of atoms stuck together. I can hardly believe sometimes in myself. The only thing that is living is not so much my body; it's my mind. And the mind is so vast that life might be as well a kind of spirit or dream. Anything is possible. I believe in anything. I believe much more in my mind than my body. My mind is open completely . . . I don't believe in time. Time is just a convention. Time is not a reality. Only my body is time. Unfortunately I have a body so I have to cope with it. My body is time, but my mind isn't time. My mind is eternity. Because I have a body I have to watch out for time.

Like all the other hippies and part-hippies, Elaine was preoccupied with time, but, as her remarks imply, she was concerned with it because of the oblique perception that somehow any conception of time was a conception of a particular relationship of mind and body. The body and the senses have their own routines and rhythms, from the full circle of life and death to the continuous beatings of the heart. The separation of thought and feeling remarked by Elaine had made possible the subordination of such bodily rhythms to the conscious routines and trajectories of the attentive mind. This was the core of the problem, although it was not the way Elaine would explain the matter. She saw the locus of the problem, but she rejected the absolute time of the body, just as she rejected for herself that full commitment to the hippie life.

In the end she could not become a hippie. Instead, she said, she would do 'something for art, something for the revolution'. In the matter of time and routine, mind and body, Elaine could see the problem that becoming a hippie resolved—and indeed feel the problem so urgently that she had to stay near to the hippies unable though she was quite to accept their resolution of it.

A somewhat similar dilemma confronted her in another matter equally central to the hippie life-style. Listen for a moment to what conviction Annette could bring to a denunciation of one form of heavy game-playing, politics. To her it represented the style of intellectuality that the dominance of thought over feeling, mind over body, made possible.

People get into politics and government and suddenly they start wanting to make wars. They get all these crazy ideas in their heads. It's all in their minds, you know? They're really getting far out. They're playing like fools with something they're not masters of at all. They should respect it, because they live from it, and instead they start fucking it all up. It's getting critical right now. That's why I say they are foolish because they can't even see that. It's the governments that do it. It's politics. Wars are made

37

by talking over the telephone. The rest of us are just pawns in the game, the poor ignorant blindfolded majority. I feel really sorry for us. But I feel even more sorry for the ones who are doing it.

Such a denunciation does not stem from rational appraisal, or not only from that. Somewhere along the line Annette had become the true believer. Of such commitment Elaine was somehow not quite capable. Like innumerable others on the fringe of the hippie world, her presence there partly stemmed from a rejection of the 'heavy' world and its ways, without her being able fully to accept and absorb the hippie solution. That solution was to 'get into your own thing', where spontaneous, intense and undissociated behaviour was presumed possible. If one rejected the forms, rules and procedures of organised society, that was the only alternative. Like a large proportion of her generation, Elaine rejected the one without being able to absorb the other. Whether this was because in some instances the unlearning process could not go far enough, or because she had not gone through those transformational experiences which we shall see were necessary conditions for fully *becoming* a hippie, it is at this stage difficult to say. The result is in some ways rather sad: unable fully to accept the hippie life, she was still alienated from straight society:

> I don't call love what you read in those magazines for women. I hate the people who stay together and play the little games, play the little games of life. Everybody is playing a little part. It's funny to look at it. I'm not going to play. But I am the one who is always getting hurt and so sometimes I pretend that I'm playing the game.

Elaine and Annette did not share the same kind of commitment, but could at least share the daily concerns of hippie life. Their interest in animistic creeds and in the occult was similar in a way, but again the differences are as instructive as the similarities. For Elaine it was a nervous sense of other and discordant realities: 'I'm psychic. When I'm with somebody I can just look at them and I can feel whatever they feel about me. Recently it's getting worse and worse.' Annette would no doubt have felt something similar, except that in her it had broadened into a calm and expansive commitment to odd mythologies such as the 'age of Aquarius' and the Tarot cards. Perhaps there was a point at which reality became so absurd and incongruent that however hard the Elaines struggled with it, the solution became to sweep it all aside and resort to the new, full and self-consistent system that Annette could glean from the Tarot cards.

> They're really beautiful things. They have human symbols. In the Tarot cards are represented about as many possibilities about what can happen in a human life—a basic amount of very important things—and they're all represented in the cards. So when you get certain cards they mean certain things out of your life. And they sort of make a story; playing with the whole idea of life, that's really very beautiful.

In their vision of the good life Elaine and Annette stood fairly close, except that Elaine was still oriented towards activity, where for Annette it was being ready and receptive that counted. One of the things Elaine claimed being with the hippies had given her was a certain knowledge of the East and a compulsive desire to visit it and to 'increase her consciousness'. In the end this compulsive approach broke down when she realised that even in this she had no idea what direction she wanted increased understanding to take. Perhaps for her, too, in the end receptivity would be all:

> I would like to increase my consciousness. That's what I'm here for: to know everything, to learn everything. That's what we are here for: to know. I don't know what I want to know: just to know. Whatever will come to me.

Certainly for Annette it had become all. She would not even speak of the East in terms as active as consciousness-expansion. All it had given that was important was a certain vision of beauty. She displayed all the time a particular receptivity to the natural world and its beauty. It may be that she discovered this beauty oddly late in life and that the compact majority always knew it and simply took it for granted. Or it may be that the majority simply does not come to know it at all. At any rate, it had further alienated Annette from the constructed world around her: the natural world for her was:

> Just so beautiful basically. That's why you go out in the city and see what people do with it, you get all sad and chewed up in your soul . . .
>
> I liked Afghanistan most. More than India. India was colonised for too long. So it's all organised. But Afghanistan has never been colonised and it's all sorts of tribes, and most of the people live in small cities. Kabul is quite small. Most of the people are nomads. They're very, very free, beautiful people.

Perhaps Elaine would make the East, and pass through some transcendental experience which would enable her to espouse the hippie life emotionally as well as mentally. At the time the prospects were not auspicious. At some point she had to break through the constraints and inhibitions that years had built up. 'All the hippies tell me', she laughed, 'is that you can easily get rid of your complexes . . . that I can do anything I fancy. But that's all they've taught me.' Perhaps sadly, it was not quite so simple. As for Eliot's Hollow Men, between the desire and the spasm, between the potency and the existence, fell the shadow: 'I admit everything. I admit pornography, orgies, homosexuality—I admit absolutely everything. Bisexuality. I wish I could do it, but I can't.'

Unless some transformation came upon her, Elaine would probably be one of those who would quickly move back into the straight world which she left only in her mind. She would herself embody and provide confirmation of that judgment on the hippie world at which she had already arrived: the hippie movement was a period of transition, and the people in it did not know where they were going nor where they had come from. They were just trying to break everything in order to stand up again.

Of heroes and martyrs If there was another possibility, it was the one Annette embodied, but it might seem unattractive. She came, it will be recalled, from the same background of upper middle-class home and Catholic convent. She had moved about Europe now for several years, from disaster to disaster: 'all ups and downs, crazy'—a life comprised of a succession of love stories, generally brief, unromantic and vanishing as though they had never been. After the first few all she wanted was to have a child, and whether the father stayed or went hardly mattered any more. Now, after years of trying, Annette was expecting a baby. 'I am flipped out, Man'; which is to say that she was deliriously happy.

To the father-to-be the matter did not appear quite so straightforward. Gordon was this community's 'dealer', though no one thought of him in such professional terms. As their source of marihuana, he had, he thought, cultivated a certain speed of thought and foot. And now this! What had he shed all institutional encumbrances for? What had he dropped out for? To have a son? It was not an easy matter, and Annette's ecstatic raptures hardly aided that decisive and sensible solution to which his disposition would naturally have inclined him. It was clear that the thought of a child did not displease him; but the thought that he thought that way clearly did. What did he think of the family as an institution? It stayed pretty cool, he would murmur, so long as everyone knew exactly what they were in it for. Which, it would seem, was what was troubling him. What complicated the matter was that his present calling seemed, oddly enough, to have brought out some natural chivalrous instincts. His van was always available, for instance, to drive distraught mothers to the Remand Centre to visit the sons who had been 'busted' by the police for smoking his hash. He was really rather soft and gentle in that way, and the fact that he had stolen the van in no way diminished a kind gesture. His friends could only watch and wait and wonder.

What life did he meanwhile lead? Like himself and his past it was typical of the hippie drop-outs of the area. That for him the family stayed pretty cool was in the first place surprising, for, without doubt, he would protest, the best period of his life began the day he split with his own family.

When I split from my parents, I had an enormous weight off my mind. When I was a kid they had this enormous thing about when I was allowed out. Crazy. Even when I was at school and would be with my friends. The fact that you couldn't say 'Right, I'll see you this evening', you had to think, 'Oh, what's daddy going to think?' There were all sorts of things like that I'd put off because I didn't like asking him because he'd make such a big thing of it. He'd say: 'Well, why do you want to go out? Well, why can't you stay in at home? You're going to miss your dinner. And haven't you got any school work to do?' All the time, this barrage, this interrogation. I really got this heavy from my father. He was always interrogating me, he always wanted to know every detail of everything I did.

Against this Gordon had rebelled to the extent that he grew his hair long and found friends who could reinforce his sense of rebellion. To him, his parents *were* conventional society, or at least his main links with it. Finally breaking with his parents *felt* like 'dropping out', in that he sensed himself breaking his last strong ties with straight society. At the time he was struggling through his first year at college, with no wish to leave it if it could possibly be avoided. When he was finally expelled there was no obviously secure foothold from which to start rebuilding, and a typical process of drift took him to the now typical day in his life which he tried to describe.

Gordon: Get up at about 10. It varies between 8 and midday depending how stoned we got the night before. Then one of the first things we do is to wander up the road to the market to buy some vegetables, fruit . . . (long, long pause)

Is that about it?

Annette: No, No.

Gordon: No. Then I usually end up making some telephone calls—to find out if I'm making any bread or not. And if I'm not then I have to do something, so I try to get some 'shit'. And if it is coming off, then I get stoned or something—or we go and visit people. It varies, all quite extraordinary.

I feel very good about not having a routine thing, where you have to do the same thing every day from 9 to 5, and that's going to be the rest of your life. I couldn't stand that, really.

What most marked Gordon's life was that it was not planned in advance and that there was no clear separation between the realms of work and leisure. He saw the importance of both questions, and that they largely defined the life he now led:

I got on the 'phone to an old friend of mine the other day and said, 'Listen, can you come up some time', and I realised on the 'phone that I was thinking in terms that he'd come up perhaps this evening, perhaps tomorrow or the next day, so that when he said, 'How about next week sometime', I kind of gasped—you know it was just something I noticed in the telephone box. So I have to see him next week. That's the first time I've planned anything a week away for a long time.

I don't think I think in terms of leisure now, because everything I do has roughly the same tone to it, simply because I don't have every day a time when I have to be somewhere else. So in fact the whole thing is just a continuum. And when it gets like that of course you have to keep quite a hold over it. I mean once you start getting stoned and everything—if you really let the whole thing run you can end up just lying in a room on a mattress all day long. So in that sense you can get more of a hold over what is happening, you can feel you're directing things more if you work.

Gordon did not try to intellectualise. The philosophical basis some hippies tried to give to their behaviour meant little or nothing to him, but in this he was more typical than them. The basic framework of behaviour was, however, similar. Gordon rejected the temporal structure and routines of an organised existence in favour of an undifferentiated living in the moment. When he saw the dangers and shortcomings it might involve, moreover, he took a particularly pragmatic approach to it. He could even accept the advantages of working, at least as a means of preventing drug-induced experience gaining too great a hold.

A few weeks after the first encounter at Carraghbay Terrace Annette and Gordon found their home the subject of a raid by police searching for drugs. The possibility was a continuing element in their lives, just as it was an accepted part of the environment in which they lived. That did not prevent it coming as an unpleasant shock, although one to which they were entirely equal. Like the old pro she was, in the split second allowed to her Annette picked up the piece of hash that was the object of the visit and dropped it delicately into her full coffee cup, almost the only thing left untouched in the course of the search. The visit was the first of many to which their friends and neighbours were to be subject over the following few weeks. Apparently it always happened at this time of the year. What was not quite apparent was whether it had for the police the ritual nature of a spring clean, or some more subtle connection with the season of the year.

It should have been apparent that a call on Annette and Gordon would be followed soon after by one on the basement of 198 Carraghbay Terrace, but Jason, Helen and their friends continued to resort there at every opportunity. The first such visit was frustrated by Jason flushing the available cannabis down the lavatory, an act full of panic and without Annette's style and aplomb. The police knew they had got near, and they needed only to wait a few hours before returning and managing, in their own way, to score. Jason was arrested. He could communicate more subtly and to greater effect with his drums than his tongue. In the course of a few minutes' exchange of words with the constables he managed through a kind of innocence to make a full and complete confession—something the police in their surprise, and also in their innocence, took for boasting, and determined should be appropriately chastised.

These were anxious days at Sophie's new flat and the flats of friends. Endless discussion went rolling deep into the night, echoing Jason's drums in their formlessness and repetition. An air of utter helplessness descended on them all. They did not know what to do; they did not know how to find out what to do; and in any case they would somehow not manage to do it. Sophie and Elaine displayed their alarm and incomprehension, but at least also an agitated sense that something ought to be done. The other girls displayed a fatalistic disinterest, and the men acknowledged the matter as entirely beyond either their aid or comfort. From having amused Sophie's idleness, they now earned from her such execrations upon their own as they would not have believed possible: 'God, I am sick of this', she would moan, 'I *wish* you would do something. Can't one of you go out and get a job?'

Days passed and nothing much seemed to happen, except Gordon driving Sophie in his van the thirty miles to the Remand Centre and giving such paternal guidance as a hopeless situation left possible. Then the centre of concern suddenly changed. Alarmed by all the strange comings and goings, by the nocturnal perambulations and the smell of incense, and some strange threat that this household and its numerous appendages seemed to hold to their settled standards, the landlord turned Sophie from her new flat at a day's notice. Such disasters always have only one outcome: there was, we might say, nowhere else to go but down, something measured in this area not by which floor one lived on, but by how many others were sleeping on it. So the scene now changed to the three rooms where Lucie and baby Jo, Maggie and daughter Sarah, Barbara and boy-friend Keith, Sophie and Helen and sometimes Elaine, and assorted other transients now lived. For the most part we shall listen to Maggie, who lived there with her young baby Sarah, the child's father having long since left in the general direction of San Francisco. Maggie supports herself on £11 per week National Assistance. If Gordon represents a characteristic type of male 'hippie', Maggie, more than Elaine or even Annette, was his female counterpart. She begins by describing her day.

Journey's end

    Maggie: I feed Sarah and get her clean, and go out into the kitchen and clean up in there. Try to get everything straight before everyone starts coming in. Because we get a lot of people here. And then we go to the park. At three o'clock I go and look after the kids over the road, who go to school, and so have quite a straight, organised day. I clean up their house and give them their dinner. Until their parents come back, and I have a smoke with them [hash], then come back here and play music or go out. I try to get some writing done, or try to get some mending done.

Lucie and her baby Jo live here with me and Sarah. Barbara and Keith—Keith is Barbara's boy-friend. He lives over here.

Barbara: Yeah, every time I can make that happen. And Sophie and Helen. And various friends who drop in to see us.

Maggie: Well, various friends are not as welcome as they used to be.

Barbara: We're cracking down. It's a human need, to have space. You need it for fucking, sleeping. Not private space, just space.

Maggie: But you're always going into your own room. You like people to knock on your door.

Barbara: Oh, that's just because we're fucking and people come in. I don't mind people coming in, but they ask me a bunch of draggy questions about where the raisin bread is, and I'm trying to get it on. I mean, I don't mind if people come in and go out, but that's why I put knock first, because I don't want to have to be conscious about raisin bread when I'm trying to make love to somebody.

Maggie: Well, the trouble is, is random people, too many random elements just crashing through. You know, we don't like to reject anybody. We don't reject people, but sometimes I get overwrought.

Barbara: About time somebody came and took away the trash.

Maggie: Hiding underneath the covers. Sometimes life is so much pressure and my head is splitting.

Barbara sings: Ah, the gipsy girl she keeps awake
by dropping Mandrax and eating snakes.
And the gipsy child, she keeps him fed,
By dancing on the roof tops to ease his head.
Fa la la-la la-la la-la la-la la-la la-la la
La la la-la la-la la-la la-la la-la la

Maggie: I've been living here about 9 months. Before that I was kicked out of a pad in Powis Square, and before that I was living in Ladbroke Grove, and before that I was in Morocco.

I got thrown out of Powis Square. The landlady was going mad there and she just sort of flung me out. So I was

46

walking down to see the people over the road. I was pregnant, and I walked past here and I met a chick coming out who said have you just been thrown out, and I had 'cause I was carrying everything, so she said why don't you live here? And I said yeah.

. . . 'cause we don't have any landlord problems. Our landlord, he's young, he's 20, and he's a friend of ours. He doesn't mind about anything.

And there's a macrobiotic restaurant nearby, which is nice. There's a little sign up in the shop about everything's been grown organically. Macrobiotic is like you don't sort of eat snacks and food through the day, you just have a meal together, and keep it in balance, and try to care for everybody, and try to control all the random elements, and try to balance them. Macrobiotics is to prepare your food and to eat just that. Enough. Not to eat too much. And to be conscious of what you're eating and drinking and if it's fucking you up, then eat more fruit or eat more fish or things like that. I don't think too many of the people down at the macrobiotic restaurant are better than other people, I mean the difference is the food. The food that most people in England eat is shit. Because they don't really care about it, and they eat fish fingers and that. But I've gone off the idea of sort of making yourself healthy and pure, because the whole society is so sick. And it's kind of impossible to be really healthy in the old Japanese way, in the middle of London, without somehow doing something very weird in your head.

How old were you when you left home?

Maggie: Oh I don't know how old I was when I left home. I'm 22 now, but it doesn't mean much—I can't always remember that I'm 22.

Sophie: She spent three years at college.

Maggie: From 18 to 21. At Oxford. I took a degree in English Literature. I used to hitch abroad. I did that every summer. While I was at college I went to Greece, Turkey, France, did that, you know, every summer, on the road. Then back into college, and try and catch up. It was very schizophrenic. And I finished it, I suppose I finished it just in case. Then I tried to work, but I couldn't get a job. I thought when you left college somehow you'd step in to some kind of millionaire career thing, and I thought, yeah, that's good because then I can do what I want to do, if I've got the money. Or if I could get a nice place to live. That's what I wanted to do. But I just couldn't get a job that paid more than £15 a week, so I split off to Morocco with 2 weeks' wages and stayed there for about 6 months, coming back through Spain and Paris . . .

I got by in Morocco while my money lasted, and then selling hash cookies, and selling my clothes. I tried not to write to my parents. I wrote to them once and they sent me £5. I tried not to ask them for money, 'cause they don't really have it anyway. My father worked for about 26 years in the same factory, and he's just about to retire. He's an industrial chemist. He's very—he was very—good. He would be very good but he's stayed there too long, and he doesn't have any degree or anything like that. So he's just kind of given up. My mother works all the time. As an accountant. She's so incredible. She's got this mass of files of accounts that she fills the whole house with.

Helen: I want a book to read in bed.

Sophie: Find a book for Helen to read. Do you want a French book?

Helen: Anything. A novel. I don't want a *Tibetan Book of the Dead*.

The cat walks in.

Sophie: I think she's done all the mice in. Did you see it yesterday? She did it again this morning. The same thing. All night long she was playing with the mouse on top of me. Running over my head, and squeaking of mice, and . . . she has to be with somebody.

Barbara sings: I've got the bourgeois blues.

        Me and my baby walk all over town,
        The man tries to put us down,
        I've got the bourgeois blues.
        Ashes to ashes, mud to mud,
        Coca Cola runs thicker than blood,
        It's a bourgeois town,
        I've got the bourgeois blues.

Me and my baby walk upstairs,
The man says we don't want no hippies here,
I've got the bourgeois blues.

There was a time when you were ambitious?

Maggie: No, I wasn't ambitious.
Sophie: Oh, sure you were ambitous.
Maggie: Well, I was flattered to get into Oxford. And I was getting quite a lot of money. You get a good grant there. But I didn't do well there. I never was ambitious. I would have liked to have done journalism.

You made a stab at getting a job as a journalist?

Maggie: No. I did. And I didn't get a job. Because to do it you have to really push, and you have to get into a really competitive thing, and I just went into it slightly and then I met the people that were in it, and they just turned me off. Completely. They were so kind of shitty, that I just didn't want to know. So I just got a job with the Civil Service. For about a month. And they told me I was too scruffy.

They didn't chuck me out, they just kept putting pressure on me, 'cause I always looked scruffy, 'cause I was always staying up all night and then going in there in the morning and then staying up all night.

I would really like to go to South America, North America, I would really like to go to Canada now, 'cause Montreal sounds very interesting. And the Prime Minister says they're legalising hash.

Have you ever thought of living—have you ever wanted to live—in any other historical era?

Maggie: Yeah, I have. I used to. I studied Old English, and I really would have liked to live at some time in the Middle Ages when you sort of had this complete kind of view of the world and everything in its place. A macrocosm and a microcosm. And everything was ordered, and your choices were so few, but I would never live any time but now. Now because it's so interesting, things are changing so quickly.

Barbara sings: The saddest thing I've ever heard, absurd,
That love is just a four-letter word.

Maggie: I've decided to live now. Especially when you've
got a baby, and the baby is growing up now. You've got
to think of more things you can do to make things nice
now. Within the present situation. I'd like to get a big
house and lots of people, and people that are working at
the same thing. Musicians, or farmers. You know, farm the
land, and make music, and sell the books, and keep the
place nice, and help everybody, and lots of kids, and sort
of let the kids have relationships with all kids—outside of
the whole set-up of the government-worker bit. Outside
of that. I've seen my parents get nowhere really, and it's
not their fault, 'cause they've worked hard. But I don't
know if it could be changed 'cause I haven't really started
to get anything set up. Do what you can yourself. Either
you're going to politically agitate, demonstrate, which—
I did that. When I was in Oxford, and before that. Or you
can drop right out and kind of pretend it's all right, but
that's no good either.

You've got to somehow work out, sort of cut out a new
alternative to show people. Because it's hard to tell people.

I demonstrated about the usual things, Vietnam, and the
Bomb, and apartheid, Biafra, and race relations in England,
and all that stuff. At the time I thought—at the time there
was such excitement and feeling, and then you'd rush
home and watch it on the television news, and think, caw,
fantastic. And your parents would just say, 'Oh, another
one of those stupid demonstrations'. And you'd say, 'I was
on it, there I am!' Of course it never really did anything,
I suppose. It works up a lot of energy in you that is just
that kind of mob aggression thing, it just makes a sort of
situation out of a problem. It doesn't really do anything
about the problem.

What about a revolution?

Maggie: Well, revolutionaries are O.K. as long as they
don't come and tell me what I'm doing wrong about the
revolution, and all that. And too many revolutionaries just
sit around and argue about the revolution. And they're

very uncomfortable and uncool to be with. And likewise—
well, it's almost a sort of age-group thing, from 18 to 21,
during which the revolution is argued.

And then there is all these kind of people that are into
yoga or the *Tibetan Book of the Dead,* and they come round
and they tell you—they tell you they've seen the Great
White Light, and they say, 'Ah, it's so groovy, that's so
beautiful' (*she is now referring to the light hanging from her
ceiling*) and you say, well that's a basket top that I put up
over the lamp and I want to try to fix up a proper lamp
shade, and they would never help you do anything, they
would just say how groovy it is, and then eat all your
bread. I mean, it's really quite nauseating, really. But it's
not, of course, I mean, it's just like enthusiasm. But I'm
more interested in people's way of life now than in what
people are saying. 'Cause that's what I'm trying to work
out. Whereas, I suppose until I had Sarah, I was very much
flipped out by what people were saying. 'Cause I wasn't
really thinking about a new way of life. Just thinking about
my ideas.

Which do you think have been the best periods of your life so far?

Maggie: Now. It's all been O.K. really.

Notting Hill, the area where Maggie and the others lived,
fans out between Ladbroke Grove and Westbourne Grove.
In so far as 'hippies, heads or freaks' concentrated anywhere in
London, it was here, and to some extent this was the centre
also of that broader and even more diffuse collection of dissent-
ing young people who represented what the popular press
called the 'Underground' and of many of the institutions and
services that represented the hip and underground communities:
Release, an advice and welfare system for people on drug
charges; BIT, an information and advice centre for young
people coming to the area; the Electric Cinema and the
macrobiotic restaurants; and *I.T.* and *Friendz* and numerous
other more ephemeral journals. The area, now and then, is
dominated by young people of the kind I have described, and
by immigrants, and as a consequence it has a transitory and unsettled air. The fine Georgian and Victorian terraces and villas

now look sad and grey, and most are now divided into small anonymous flats, often owned by equally anonymous landlords, glad to live a healthy distance from the area. It is thus far removed, in everything except geography, from the area to which we now move: the Piccadilly area of Central London.

SCENE W.I

Life at the centre

The centre, then, is pre-eminently the zone of the sacred, the zone of absolute reality. Similarly, all other symbols of absolute reality (trees of life and immortality, Fountain of Youth etc.) are also situated at a centre. The road leading to the centre is a 'difficult road' (durohana) and this is verified at every level of reality; difficult convolutions of a temple (as at Borobudur); pilgrimage to sacred places (Mecca, Hardwar, Jerusalem); danger-ridden voyages of the heroic expeditions in search of the Golden Fleece, the Golden Apples, the Herb of Life; wanderings in labyrinths; difficulties of the seeker for the road to the self, to the 'centre' of his being, and so on. The road is arduous, fraught with perils, because it is, in fact, a rite of the passage from the profane to the sacred, from the ephemeral and illusory to reality and eternity, from death to life, from man to the divinity. Attaining the centre is equivalent to a consecration, and initiation; yesterday's profane and illusory existence gives place to a new, to a life that is real, enduring and effective.

So Mircea Eliade (1954, p. 17) on the symbolism of the centre in archaic societies.

London is the centre of England. And Piccadilly Circus is the centre of London. What journeys to Afghanistan and Nepal meant for some of our informants, moving to the Piccadilly area meant for others. Each was a way of searching for some inner self, some absolute self at the centre of one's being.

Piccadilly gained this role not just because it was a city centre but because, like many other kinds of centre, it was the meeting ground of extremes. Half-way between the National Gallery and the Royal Academy, it is dotted with pornographic book-shops. In the early evening the neon lights are there the most pervasive and insistent. In the early morning the streets are that little more full of rubbish and garbage sacks and dustbins. It is a showcase for luxury and a resort for the vagrant and dispossessed. Life starts there later in the morning than else-where and ends there later at night. City centres are normally considered the highest expression of a civilisation, the focus of its culture and art, yet seem also to draw to themselves its excesses of depravity and violence. They are the heart of social and festive life and also the anomic resort of all who would loose human ties, an identity or a name. Like Annette's Tarot cards, Piccadilly thus poses all the alternatives that a life may hold.

For most people it remains, however, the land of make-believe, for escape once a year, or once every few months, and for only very few even in the London region more often. It provides excitement, and ministers to the need for occasional cathartic release of those emotions and tensions which may find no outlet in the round of everyday life. Its business, in a way, is the intensification of experience, and it does it in-cessantly. But who is in the West End all the time? The majority come only infrequently, to the theatres and shows, just often enough to puncture the settled routines of their life, without upsetting its essential balance. Even the actors and strippers, the booksellers and waitresses, mostly beat a nightly retreat by last tube or taxi to twilight zones outside the centre, where they may salvage their other selves.

Only to the likes of Jimmy and Sue and Ben is it home all the time. It is a home to people like these trying to find themselves, and we shall see that it is appropriate for this purpose just because its business is the intensification of experience. Jimmy, Sue and Ben are our guides through this second world. Jimmy is a 'speed freak', Sue a former junkie still partly dependent on heroin. Ben, who sets the scene for us, is any other Piccadilly hippie. They are part of that group of young people whom the dominant society encounters at two points: as tourists it photographs them as they sprawl languidly on the steps of Piccadilly Circus by day, and as theatre-goers it stumbles in alarm upon them in alley-ways as they lie in the shadows of night. Jimmy, relatively new to the scene, is immersed in it and seldom experiences any other reality; Sue, an older hand, though still predominantly involved in it, has moved a few steps out and stabilised a few links to the dominant order. Before we enter their private worlds let us briefly show where they fit in.

They were numbered among the hippies forming part of the drifting population of the West End, whose numbers varied at different times of the year, but which must at least have numbered several hundreds and at times must have numbered several thousands. Of those who were under twenty-five, and thus my concern, it was estimated that some 70 per cent were boys; and that almost 35 per cent were aged sixteen to eighteen, 40 per cent aged nineteen to twenty-one and 25 per cent aged twenty-one to twenty-five.[1] Almost all had experienced some personal disaster in adolescence or before. 90 per cent had left school at fifteen or sixteen. Almost three-quarters had appeared in court on some charge or other. And, most important of all, three-quarters were using drugs of some kind regularly and at least one quarter were registered drug addicts. Those who were not briefly in accommodation of their own or temporarily accommodated by some social agency were spending the nights in clubs or cafés, walking the streets or in the park. The large majority did not work, other than casually. Except for a lucky few who with some recognised accommodation were able to obtain social security, most had only such money as they could acquire in ways Jimmy and Sue will describe. During the day those who did not have any employment sat in the parks or squares when it was fine, retreated to day-centres when it was wet or when they were in need of help. It was in one of the squares that we met Ben, for a moment a little away from the dust and noise.

Ben, a Piccadilly hippie Ben had just come out of prison. As a consequence his hair was close-cropped, giving him a boyish look more in keeping with his age than almost every other aspect of his appearance. Although only eighteen he must have been nearer seven than six feet tall. He had blondish hair and a lightly tanned complexion, which broke every few minutes into an innocent and disarming grin. He wore the ubiquitous blue jeans, tattered and patched, and khaki army surplus shirt, and over these a full-length sleeveless fur coat: if it had seen better days, it had at least probably never received the unending and devoted use it now had from its present owner. But it was his height which marked Ben out as different, as indeed it always had. It left its own mark on every aspect of his life, and seemed to condition his every movement.

I use Ben to describe the way of life of the West End hippie. He was in no sense special. He was typical in that he came into this kind of life through alienation and insecurity, in this case following the break-up of his home: in the manner of his exclusion from the broader society and attachment to the 'hip scene' which I shall analyse in the next chapter; in the opposition to straight society that mirrored his conflict with his parents; and in his distaste for 'The King's Road type, Chelsea, the Ravers, Weekend hippies', who flirt with the bohemian life but do not really live it. Such factors will become important as this study progresses, but what is important here is how well he illustrates the two characteristic patterns in the life of the West End hippie. They were the distinguishing features also of the life of the Ladbroke Grove hippies. One was attachment to the values, attitudes and life-style which we have already heard Maggie and her friends articulate. The other was a daily life even more disordered and unpremeditated than theirs.

Ben described first of all his purposeless mode of daily living. It was spring, and he was not looking forward to the season:

The last couple of years I enjoyed it. I'm not sure I'm going to enjoy it this year. Maybe it's because it's a bit early —summer hasn't really started yet. Last year you could sleep in the Park and they didn't bother you—they used to wake you up and tell you to move on first thing in the morning, but now you can't even go to sleep.

A lot of the tourists just come to see us. They hear about the hippies in London—I used to make all my money that way—they pay you to take your photograph.

We used to hang around down the crypt—St Martin's in the Field. Everyone used to hang around there during .the day—just sit around there. It's a pretty sick place now— I know I'd never go back. It's all old men.

The Dilly scene, people hanging around the Dilly, it's

dying off very very quickly. I'm inclined to believe that perhaps the law are winning. Where's everybody going to go—very few heads on the Dilly now. You get about ten hanging around outside the Pronto Bar. Before there were a couple of hundred of them. We used to sit in the Dilly all day.

I sleep down the Embankment now because the bread scene's pretty low—in fact the bread scene's nil and I get a meal down there every night. They bring a soup wagon round—there's soup and food and I sort of fill myself up with food and that lasts me till the following night. Up until last night though I was crashing with a friend. But the landlord got uptight about it and threw us all out.

There's only one thing I get bored about—I'm bored until the food comes round, and then I'm happy! That's my one hang-up on the road.

I think it's going to be bad this summer. Last summer I was going with a chick and people used to take pity on the girl so we used to get plenty of money for food.

To most people it would seem little short of hell, but from Ben it elicited no such clear reaction. He could not be happy with his life, but, as we heard him describe in the previous chapter, hell for him was represented rather by the deadening repetition of the 9 to 5 work routine.

In stark contrast to this earthy life, pursued all the time at a low level of consciousness, were the elements of his hip ideology which by comparison must seem sublime and somewhat ridiculous. His hold upon them may have been tenuous but his commitment was persistent and uncompromising. Having had a broken educational history and left school young, he was not now an avid reader, but when he did read it was R. D. Laing, or 'a guy called Alan Watts'. He would honestly admit that he did not understand a word of it, but at least it became a little clearer under acid. Also he was, like Maggie, on a 'sort of health food thing', as a vegetarian, but since he was, as we saw, penniless and hungry a good proportion of the time, the principle had to be honoured in a rather negative way. He was also interested in Yoga and Buddhism 'just from an in-trip point of view', and subscribed to the primal vision of hippie

56

life—the commune—and on the few occasions he could drag himself from the self-torture of Central London, it was to something like this that he would go. Here he could briefly act out the hippie vision. Even here, however, there yawned a schism between ideal and reality: his use of the word 'commune' comes to appear simply a subscription to the vision. The reality was very different and hardly fitted any normal definitions of the word. This disparity is not, however, important. What mattered was the experience.

> I was down in Cornwall for a while and we had a commune down there. Well, I say a commune, me, this chick and her three kids, and we were growing our own food as far as possible. We were growing vegetables and potatoes. We used to go out and buy rice and just the bare essentials. We used to make our own bread and we had this cottage, we paid 30/- a week for it—admittedly I was on the dole. I used to get ten quid a week, which wasn't a lot to keep a girl.
>
> She was really turned on and we used to get rice and we made our own bread: there was no gas, no electricity, no running water: there was a fresh-water well, literally outside the back door, with all these little worm things that keep the water clean. You could drink straight out of the bucket.
>
> We used to get a big calor gas thing and there was a range stove, we used to go out and get wood for that and we used to get bamboo and make dragons for flutes and get a bit of wire and heat it up—you could just get a bit of wire and push it around and make a nice pattern: we used to sell them down at Mevagissey, down in Cornwall. It was really nice down there. Now I'm back on the road again.

Ben was a follower of fashion. He had absorbed the hip life-style, and adjusted to its changes, because it was the only sort of identity he found himself able to sustain. In the context of the life that he had to pursue from day to day, the 'commune' in Cornwall, health foods, Yoga and even Alan Watts are bound to take on a somewhat insubstantial air, but Ben believed in them. And for all their fragility, they had at least attractiveness

57

and some sort of consistency. This was more, Ben felt, than did his life before attaining the centre, a life whose wounds still littered his memory: the broken home, the alcoholic father who attacked drug use; the authorities who always called joy rides 'taking and driving away', and any sort of knife an offensive weapon.

Ben came repeatedly back to London and stayed there in the summer for many reasons. One was that it was probably only there that he could get food and occasional shelter from begging and charity. Another was that he had the support of others like himself. A third was that it was as near as possible to the source of the hippie vision. It was the centre. The 'commune' in Cornwall may have provided an opportunity to act out the vision: but to be at the source and origin of this vision, that was something more. Fundamentally, however, his reason for returning was, in the words used by many informants, that London was where the life was. London held open the possibility of intensified experience. It did this because it was the most convenient source of drugs; because it is the centre for music and underground clubs. It was this that kept Ben in London. The origin and significance of the commitment to intensified experience will appear a recurring theme of this study. What are its contexts in the hippie way of life?

When we turn from Ben to Jimmy and Sue, we see the various ways in which, for the hippie, intensified experience could link to, and provide contrast with, the rest of their lives. We encounter Jimmy in one of the day centres for young people in trouble. He is on 'speed'—that is amphetamine. The problem of the moment, apart from continual brushes with the police, is that it is raining.

Jimmy: the journal of a speedfreak

I have been around the West End two or three years. Once you come to the West End you can't really leave the place. If you go maybe to a new town it is just a fucking drag, you know.

I just hang around the Dilly. And then sometimes I fancy a break and I go to the country. I work hard and get some bread and then I go to the country for a break, because

London does piss you off a bit: the fuzz, you know, they are real bastards, they just keep moving you on.

My home used to be in Portsmouth, but my parents are split up. I don't like living there because it is just a drag. You know what I mean? I don't fancy just sitting there looking at tele. I would rather be out in the street looking around. Around the Dilly you see all the people, and you can laugh at them. Last week I drew about eight pictures. I tried to sell them. Sometimes they sell. I used to do portraits for a living around the centre of London, for the tourists you know.

When I first left Portsmouth I went off along the coast just living in barns and sleeping. I just went alone. It was good. I could just do what I wanted. If I didn't like the scene I could move. But now it is all fucked up. A couple of years ago it was pretty good, but now you are just like a robot walking the streets.

Older people these days, they just don't know anything. They just get up at 8.00 every morning and they go to work until they drop dead. And you know that is not it. That is not where it is at.

Have I ever had a job? Yes, 70 or 75, I have had all different kinds. I can't remember what the last one was it was too long ago. Well, I did work in a holiday camp. That was good because when we were finished we could just go down by the sea. Then once I was supposed to do packing for a guy at a desk. I lasted half an hour and then I pissed off. I don't believe in work. Well, you can work and by the time you work all week you get £15 and after that the Government and those shits at Westminster take most of it away from you. I know what it is about really. Work is important for most people now, because the majority of people are sick.

It is better the way it is now. When I need bread I can just go out and sell shit for someone and that gives me bread. I used to get £130 a week in the West End, but then the fuzz moved in and they cut me off. Now I only get a few pounds, get stoned and go to sleep.

I suppose I am a dealer. I don't like heroin though. I don't sell it too much. I have never used it. I take a lot of acid. Well, I used to take a lot of acid. But after a while it just fucks you up.

And I like speed. You do a lot of talking and while you are talking you are making bread, and you have a nice time, too. You get it into your system and then you want to—ah—well you know it is good stuff. If you are speeding it makes you more active so that when you want to do something you do it. So if you are speeding you go out and do more things. That is why I like speed. Maybe if you take about 20 a day, in the night time say, well in the morning you are feeling a bit fucked up. So you just have to sleep it off. I take about thirty a time. It is a good buzz.

I smoke shit every day of the week. And I drink every day of the week. I have got a bottle out there. I drink cider and whisky.

There was a drug scene in Southampton when I was 15. But I didn't get into the scene then. I just drifted into smoking. When I was 15. I left home then you know and I just went along the beach and I met these long hair fuckers and they had shit and they said 'Here man, take a draw'. I did, you know, and I felt very dizzy—but after a while it got to be pretty good so I started using it every day.

Did I think about using drugs before I began? I don't know. You just sort of drift into it. You start using a lot and if you don't stop then you end up an addict—that is fucked up by the way. I don't really like needles. Maybe if it was just pills I would be like them.

Drugs make you fucking lazy, I will tell you that. If you keep getting stoned and using speed then you stay out late at night and you don't get any sleep. Then during the day-time you just lay there all day. But now I want to get some energy so that I can do things.

I like to do things I like. Well, I was relaxing out there. I would have been lying there all day if you hadn't come along and wanted to talk. Usually I am running around so today I decided to relax. I have been in Scotland for five days looking at the mountains and that changes you, you know.

Well, you know, if you are in a city it is not real. If you are in the country you have got the sheep there, and you and the sky, and it is nice. You can talk to the people when you are in the country. You don't see too many and when you do see them you can speak to them.

Is there anything I don't like about using drugs? It is up to the person who uses them. It is not forced on to you, you don't get it unless you want it. I have changed since I started using drugs. I think it is much better. I am just doing what I want to do.

I don't think I will always use drugs. I just like to play around with it. When I have bread I have these parties. They go on for about three days. First we all smoke, then we drink, then people drop acid, and then wow, we all blow our minds. After that you have some friends and some who don't care for you at all. It can get pretty rough at these things. You just can't control it. With acid, you know, your eyesight, your bones, the whole works, it just blows your head off, the things you can see. Like now you walk out to the street and you just walk along and you don't take much notice, but on acid the noises, the colours, it is all too much. If you get good acid then you really have a nice trip, but most acid I have had, well—mind blowers as my friend says.

. . . I like people, but not very many of them. I have got two friends. One of them is in prison and one of them I will see this afternoon. And the rest, well, I do what I want, you know. I have been in prison, and remand when I was 13. For stealing, offensive weapons (*laugh*) well that is about it, but I have done it a lot of times. It is a fucking drag sitting in a cell, boxed up. I forget when I was last in prison. Oh you forget a lot when you take shit and speed. You only live for now and you fuck the rest.

I get up in the morning and go out and get some bread and tonight I will go to the pub. I have a nice time really. If I want to I can just go to sleep for about three weeks and then when I wake up I will have it all sorted out.

It used to be that I was after a gold Rolls Royce. I would hustle all this bread and I was trying to save it up, but I couldn't save it, I would just spend it. It is easy to hustle bread. You go down to the Dilly and, well, it isn't very nice, are you sure that you want to hear? It is mean the way I do it. I wouldn't like to tell you about it. I would like to keep it because it, well a lot of people know already and they are just stupid and they tell the fuzz. And the fuzz don't want no long hairs earning their bread.

Well, you just ask the tourists if they want to buy some shit and if they want some, then you take them around the corner with a knife and you say hand over your bread and then you split fast. Sometimes you have to slam them over the head. I couldn't care less. I need bread, fuck them. I never asked to be put here, that is the way I look at it.

I just do what I want all the time. I am not looking for something to do in ten years. Today is today. The world might blow up for all we know. I just wake up today and do what I want to do. We never planned for the future, only that I have always been drawing. When I came out of school I took the wrong choice. A job for me could have been sign writing—that is painting—but I took this other job which was leather cutting and I got all fucked up. So I went back after this other job but it was gone. So I started all these different jobs. Really I should have stuck to painting and I would have been a straight bastard, but I started smoking shit instead and now I am a street bastard, and that's that. I don't like straight people. They just bug me.

For me black magic is where it's really at. I want to get it going there. A lot of long-hairs are in to this black magic. It's really weird. You can get things that just come out of the ground. But I'm a bit of a nosey bastard. I want to find out about it. The more you read of it, and you sit back for a day and just think about what you just read, and then you read some more and gradually it gets a grip on you, and you're running around all the libraries and learning more about it. And there are quite a few people, you know, they're mad and they're locked up. I don't think they should be locked up—only because of the fuzz and shit—that again.

My parents do not care—well only my mother you know. Every three or four months when I get bread and clean clothes I go to see her and leave her some bread. Before I go I like to get looking very smart, because my mother is nice and all.

In the summer of 1970 Jimmy would have been labelled a 'speedfreak' within the circles in which he moved. This was the term to describe young people who persistently use amphetamines in preference to other drugs. Among West End hippies there were many of them. This relationship to amphetamines obviously determines a large part of his experience and behaviour. With a proper dispassion the Advisory Committee on Drug Dependence has set on record (1970) what habitual consumption may involve, at least as it appears to the conventional observer:

> The patients are often restless, irritable and antisocial. Later rapid speech and verbal aggression are common and overt aggression may occur. Involvement with crime is described and accident proneness has been reported because overconfidence leads to lack of care and because of ataxia. Other patients describe a cleaning-up 'mania' or 'getting hung up' on an activity such as cleaning a wall, which they continue to do for hours.

Between this description and Jimmy's own experience there were many similarities. It was not a matter, however, that this pattern of living was the unsought consequence of his having been fortuitously 'hooked' on the drug. Nor would it be right to conclude that outside his dependence on amphetamines, his experience and behaviour were random and without clear meaning and structure. In fact, quite the opposite was true: just because Jimmy was such an extreme case, he clearly exhibited the fundamental pattern of experience and behaviour that in some measure characterised all my informants. In any case, people generally took drugs because of specific effects they produced, or were believed to produce, directly or indirectly. Jimmy was certainly right when he remarked: 'It is up to the person who uses drugs. It is not forced on to you: you don't get it unless you want it.'

Jimmy wanted it, he said, because it changed the tone and pitch of his experience: if you are taking amphetamine, when you want to do something, you just go out and do it. The rules and precepts of life in an advanced industrial society—rational, purposive activity, restraint and the deferral of gratification were undermined. The cultural paraphernalia of dissociated sensibility, the lags and buffers between the three facets of human experience, thought, emotion and action, were dissolved. On the one hand his account reveals his inability or unwillingness to plan, and even to act rationally and purposefully.

> I just do what I want all the time. I just wake up today and do what I want to.
>
> It used to be that I was after a gold Rolls Royce. I would hustle all this bread and I was trying to save it up, but I couldn't save it, I would just spend it.

On the other hand, it reveals a special pattern of living: long periods of intensive activity followed by long periods of complete relaxation. A three-day long party was followed by a three-day long sleep. Long periods of indolence and inactivity alternated with feverish and obsessive bursts of activity. By contrast with the conventional pattern of mild work followed by mild leisure, Jimmy carried each to extreme.

Jimmy seemed to value his drug condition and the pattern of life derived from it because of the elimination of the barriers between thought, emotion and action. So far as was possible Jimmy's behaviour became spontaneous and reflexive: the thought was embodied almost immediately in the action. There was no lag or buffer between them as in normal rational activity. And in such activity, however absurd or mundane, Jimmy showed a kind of emotional absorption. It may be that the breaking of the barriers between thought, emotion and action was the goal in itself or it may have been the means to a different goal: from the breaking of such barriers and the sort of behaviour flowing from it may have been forged such sense of personal identity and unity as Jimmy had. At very least his experience of himself as a person was intensified. It is somehow in keeping with such intensified immediate experience that the extent to which the categories of past and future impinged upon him was diminished: the present wipes out the future as well as the past.

This was the basic structure of life that all my subjects sought and followed, although it did not always become as patent as in Jimmy's case. Jimmy also illustrates other habits and attitudes that hippies of W.11 or W.1 shared that were derived from this particular way of modulating and intensifying experience. The first was the way the process had made his everyday environment 'unreal'. At bottom this was because the transcendence of dissociated sensibility excluded him from a social order dependent upon it. The drug may have intensified his experience and given him a 'nice time', but the cost was his inability to relate to the temporal routines and regularities of the dominant society: if he kept getting stoned and using speed, he stayed out late at night and did not get any sleep and consequently would have been unable to join the 8.oo a.m. march to work, even if he had felt inclined to. It was perhaps fortunate therefore that he regarded the people who did this as 'sick'. There was little substantial difference between Jimmy in Piccadilly Circus and Gordon in Ladbroke Grove, protesting how good he felt at not having a routine thing. For both, instead of the conventional daily routine repeated through the week, long periods awake were succeeded by long periods of sleep, with daily cycles quite irrelevant: with no conventional social activity operating on that cycle they were forced, almost by that fact alone, to be outsiders. For this reason, and because of the periodic intensity of their personal experience, Jimmy saw the rhythms of life in the dominant society from the viewpoint of the outsider, who gazed on them from a distance and could not directly experience them. 'In a city it is not real', he said, 'and the people going off to work must be sick.'

Excluded from the conventional framework of social behaviour, Jimmy fell prey to the kind of animism that the outsider's sense of the unreality of the dominant society almost inevitably induces. More than two-thirds of those people interviewed at length in the West End subscribed to some mystical or magical creed of an animistic form. They seldom had the sophistication and complexity that Elaine, Annette and their friends gave to theirs, but their origin and significance were similar.

Jimmy's account is important in that it shows the full spectrum that the 'hip scene', in London at least, covered: it moved from the rarefied heights of the seekers after truth of Ladbroke Grove to the raw and torn life of the city-centre hippies. Whatever distance was traversed, from Annette and Gordon to Ben and Jimmy, the same themes recurred, as they do also in the self-portrait of Sue, the last person we meet in this excursion.

Sue: between two worlds   Sue was short and rather fat, and sported an expensive leather coat. She was a former heroin addict, and shared the same friends .and haunts as Ben and Jimmy. She was representative of large numbers of troubled and disturbed people on the edge of hippie society. Her lesbianism and her early use of 'pills' drew her almost inevitably to Central London and to involvement with the hippie scene. She identified with that scene, however little it would accept her as representative of it. In her own tiredness and failure she now saw reflected the failure of the 'scene'. It was destined to fail, she claimed, because of the newspapers 'exaggerating and slanderising its activities from 1964 onwards'. Almost a feeling of martyrdom came through as she protested that the previous generation of beatniks, among whom her parents were numbered, had no such 'aggravation', but she still managed to see herself as one of the survivors.

Her life was pursued half in the hip world, and half in the straight, and it was this perhaps that left her a survivor. She had once been enmeshed in the way of life which Jimmy pursued, but when she found it too much she had moved halfway back and stabilised some links with the conventional world of work and leisure. But she could not go all the way back: she might no longer be hooked on heroin, but she was still hooked on the intensification of experience. From time to time she had still to kick over the traces, and go off to the centre 'to find life', but it was her enduring anchors in the straight world that she described first.

I work at a hotel in Kensington. I run the cocktail bar there. I live there. The man I work for is OK and the pay is good because I have no expenses. The customers are great too. Sometimes I keep them talking to me all night. They must think I am goofy. I open and close the bar when I want to. They must think I keep funny hours. Sometimes when I close the bar at 2 a.m.—sometimes I close at 11 p.m.—sometimes when I close at 2 I go dashing out. I know I can always find life in London any time of day. I am a lesbian and I like the gay scene. I know where to go any time of night to find life. Sometimes I go dashing out at 2 and come stumbling back in as the doorman opens in the morning. He must think I am funny.

I ran a cocktail bar once before and I liked that. The thing is, though, I don't like the responsibility. I worked in a deaf school once. I liked the work but it made me feel guilty. All those poor kids. I had so much and they didn't have anything. It made me feel guilty and I used to cry all the time. Then they found out that I was on morphine and I had to quit. But I didn't like that job really because there was too much responsibility. I want a nice job, something soft, but I don't want any responsibility. I don't know how much longer I will stick this job. I like sticking a job usually—I've been at this job nearly a year. I like the security.

I would work even if I didn't need the money—for a separation. Only for a few hours maybe, but it is a bit of reality which I need. You need a few hours stability. Working breaks up the crazy periods. It helps one get outside the scene for a few hours. I don't like working but it gives me an independence and stability which I need for this scene. There's never been a period when I haven't worked—well, except for three months when I was too bad fix wise to know what was going on. Then I just hung around the Dilly all day. That was a couple of years ago when I was using so much heroin that I couldn't work. I didn't know anything then. I didn't know what was going on time wise.

I used to work for a clip joint then in Soho for a few hours a day, a bar where prostitutes go. You pick up someone, get the money off him and then get lost without going through with it. There are hundreds of them around here in Soho. I did that for a couple of months. Oh, yes, and I know what made that period go by. I found a second father. A really great guy. He was rich—he owned a lot of clubs and bars around here and had houses all over London. I met him in one of his bars. I was just sitting there and he made friends with me. He took care of me and gave me a room in one of his houses. At two o'clock every night I would meet him and he would take me home—just drop me there and give me a pound to get back to the Dilly the next day. I wouldn't know what time it was all day—but somehow at 2 a.m. something would click and say go meet X and he would take me to the house where I lived with the housekeeper. Then about noon the next day something would click again and say, 'It's time to head for the Dilly'. He was a really great guy. He didn't want anything from me and he didn't even like drug addicts at all. He just thought I had a certain sparkle which he liked.

He was a poor cockney who had made it lucky. He had all that money and he still used to work. For about three hours every night he would go up to Oxford Street to one of the cafés which he owned and work. He said he needed it. He would just work in the kitchen or something. He said he needed it to keep himself straight. I still see him some-times. He took me to the races last week, and I sent him a fabulous kind of Christmas card at Christmas, but it is not the same as it was. It's not the same because now I have a job and can take care of myself. We just are not on the same wavelength as we once were.

I have always earned my own money. It is important to be independent. I have been able to do a lot this last year because I make good money and have few expenses. Everything I have now I have bought in the last year from this job. I had a lot of things before but when I was on methedrine I sold it all to get the drug—diamond rings my mother had given me, a beautiful gold cross, coats, everything I had I sold to get the drug. They did away with the drug. They took it off the market. You can't even score for it. You just can't find it. If it were around I would be scoring for it. It is the most beautiful drug. I had to go off it because it just wasn't available any more. Now I have got some nice things again. But I would sell them all again if I could get methedrine. It is such a beautiful drug—the most beautiful drug—it makes me sick that it is not around any more. My parents don't give me things any more because they were so upset when I sold it all for drugs. They won't give me a thing now.

I have always lived somewhere in London. My parents

were theatrical, my father is a trumpet player and my mother is a dancer—she still has the best figure, she is still so thin—and I was born in Maida Vale. My parents are so groovy. We really get along well. I really like them. My father is retired now and they live down Bournemouth. We're pretty broke now though—it has always been the same—we have always been pretty broke. But we are going to sell the house and get a smaller one. Then we will be OK. But my father always bought these fantastic things. He used to come home at night after work with fantastic presents. One time he brought me a fabulous two-wheeler. Blue I think. We never asked him where he got the things and he never said. I am a thief. I steal from shops—I didn't steal this coat, I bought it. And I bought this jumper, but I stole all the rest—my handbag and everything in it. I just walk in and steal things.

My father steals too—we understand each other. Theatrical people know what is going on.

I see my parents once a week. I go down there. Sometimes my mother takes a couple of pills with me. She is too much—she takes them and she can do the housework—all herself. She runs around cleaning. When I take four times as many I am still knocked out—I still can't do anything. I just lie around.

I have been on drugs all my life. I was popping pills in school when I was 13. But I can moderise it now. I don't really miss drugs except methedrine. I keep barbiturates around—just like I keep a bottle of whisky—for security. Just so that I will know that they are there if I need them.

I misused school. I wish I could go back. I was really detached from school because I was on pills. I mean I would take a pill and then I just wouldn't be there any more. I didn't like the kids. They seemed so young. It was funny because the teacher used to think that I was the ringleader. That was so silly. Because I was on pills I didn't want anything to do with the other kids. But she used to blame all the trouble on me. There was nothing wrong with school, it was me—that was why I didn't like school. You see, I was precocious. I used to go around with my older brother and sisters a lot. I would see the things that they would do and then the kids my age—the kids at school—would bore me. I went to the jazz clubs with my brother and would see the kids there doing things and then I would do them too.

I was kicked out of secondary modern school and sent to approved school. It was great. I loved it. There were only twenty girls there, you could do courses and exams. They treated us very well. I liked the security, the people there were semi-respectable and I liked that, and I liked the girls—I liked having them around because I am a lesbian. I was there eighteen months and when they told me it was time for me to leave I didn't want to go. I didn't want to leave the security. Once I went back to visit after I had left. That time the headmistress had to kick me out. I made such a scene when it was time to leave that she told me that I could never come back. I came out of approved school in 1967. I was also in a psychiatric hospital. I was there for eighteen months and I came out about a year ago. I liked it there too. It did me a lot of good. We did group discussions and that kind of thing. I wish I had stayed longer. It would have done me more good. We all helped each other there. It was a great place. I liked the security there too.

When I first came out of approved school I worked as a seller for a textile firm. I worked with some crazy and really nice old men. I used to take days off and they wouldn't say anything. Then I moved in with my brother and we both got hooked on methedrine—I got him hooked —and I quit the job. Then one day he kicked me out because he got fed up. He quit his job, sold everything he had—all the beautiful things he had in his apartment— took his trumpet and went down to Cornwall to live. He plays the trumpet just like my father. He kicked the drug. He just figured out what it was all about and realised that he wasn't living the right way. So he sold everything and moved out.

Now I just go around with my friends to the bars and coffee bars and things. I like eating and talking and seeing my friends.

I don't spend much time thinking about what I am going to do in the future, making plans and that sort of thing.

I have got a restlessness though. I want to do something new—meet some nice people. I know a lot of people on the gay scene and I am always getting rolled. I got rolled by a friend over the weekend. He rolled me and robbed me. What could I do? I just had to smile it off. But I am getting tired of it and I want to meet some nice people. That is why I want to do something different. I won't meet nice people in London. I don't know what or where but it would have to be out of London.

Sue may find her way back into straight society. At the time of the study she hovered on the margin. She felt old and tired from the strain of a life outside the rhythms and routines of the dominant social order, with few of the supports it conventionally provides. At bottom she wanted to go straight and she saw that this meant leaving London, leaving the centre. Although she did not like working, she acknowledged that it was only in regular work that some sense of contact with reality resided. She was fortunate in her job. She was necessarily to some degree an outsider by the fact that her lesbianism and her involvement in the London drug scene dictated routines and time schedules at variance with society's: she sensed that it was in this that she was most vulnerable to the curiosity and mild deprecation of the straight people—the customers who must have thought her goofy for keeping them talking all through the night and the doormen who must think her funny for coming stumbling back as they opened the hotel in the morning. But so long as the fact of a job gave her some tenuous hold on reality and so long as it was of the sort that provided some justification for her pattern of living, she could pursue in relative safety her search for life. This she would no doubt do as long as belief and enthusiasm survived.

She was different in that she was more stable than most hippies, at any rate those of the West End. The reader will have seen that she was similar in many other ways. For our purposes two particularly stand out. She echoed Jimmy and every other outsider whom we have followed in a belief that in some sense the dominant society is not real. Theatrical people, she remarked, know what is going on: beneath the level of everyday reality, other more fundamental and real currents are moving, which

71

only the outsider, detached from the dominant system, can perceive.

That very word 'detached', which she used to describe herself and which for so many hippies expresses their feeling towards the dominant society, reveals the second similarity. In her case, it was not so much in lesbianism, pursuit of the gay life, or previous psychological troubles that her condition as outsider found origin. Rather it was that in her school days, when she was using pills, she was detached from everything, 'not there anymore', and through her precocity out of step with the other children. It is partly by such disjunctions between the rhythms of the individuals' private world and those of his social environment that bohemian outsiders are made.

III

TRANSFORMATION: BECOMING
A HIPPIE

Usually people from the outside just see dirty, long-haired hippies—drug-taking, sex orgies and all that. Well, maybe you do go through that stage at the beginning. But there's something more you can't explain: I'd go so far as to say that with these people there's a certain sort of difference. There's a kind of line between these people and the rest. There's a kind of image, a kind of thing that they understand more than anyone else does—the idea of life.

Nick was a new arrival on the 'hip scene'. He viewed it from the inside, because he felt that he had *become* a hippie, but he was still new enough to it to recall something of what it looked like from the outside. He liked the way hippies lived, he asserted, and he liked to live that way. But that was not all. There was, he believed, a special image that they followed and a secret knowledge that guided them. About the vision and the knowledge there was, it was always suggested, something bordering upon the mystical and sacred. That these elements may have been largely self-delusion is not important: for some reason which we must examine, the novitiate hippie believed the illusions, acted them out. In the process he gave them reality.

These elements in the process of becoming what the world would call a hippie are rather special and are the main concern of this chapter. They are inextricably linked, however, with two more familiar factors. The first is the identity crisis of youth, and the second is those everyday social processes which tend gradually to confine an individual to a deviant identity once he has first espoused its proscribed habits and values: by a thousand slight gestures and shades of meaning, the person involved in drug-taking, sex orgies or even originally just long hair comes to be labelled as 'hippie', and comes himself to accept the limitations of that label. It is a sort of mental shorthand: a *does* b, c, d, etc., therefore a *is* x, a hippie or whatever. The label once attached, the box is sealed almost irrevocably. Such processes are at work in the creation of all kinds of deviant identity. In the case of the hippie, however, they were perceived and experienced in a special way: they were felt to be the mundane mechanics of an essentially moral and spiritual process. Becoming a hippie was experienced as a kind of total transformation, which the young person half-knowingly brought upon himself. At a certain point the individual made an inductive leap. Becoming a hippie may have been partly a process of daily action and reaction, but it was ultimately necessary that the individual see visions and dream dreams, and finally *will himself to become a hippie*.

How these two elements linked and worked themselves out, and the way in which they influenced and permeated the young person's perceptions and experience once he had become a hippie, is the subject of this chapter. I shall illustrate it first of all by some observations on the history of the hippies we met in the last chapter, most of whose transformations were long passed. I shall then elaborate it by reference to Nick and three other young people who had recently come into contact with these sub-cultures and who were in the throes of becoming hippies.

OUTSIDERS

One preliminary matter requires comment. To understand properly the processes that bring about change, it is necessary first to appreciate the nature and extent of the change involved. There was, said Nick, a *kind of line* between those who had become hippies and those who had not. What did this involve?

In the previous chapter I have from time to time used the term 'outsiders' to express the presence of such a line. It has an obvious relevance to our theme. This derives from the fact that the word has an established place in the study of deviance to express a subtle ambiguity in the relationship of a society and a deviant minority: members of a deviant minority may feel themselves outsiders to the 'compact majority', but they

themselves make members of that majority feel outsiders by
the private language and signs which they develop to communicate only with their own kind.

It has, however, a more haunting relevance. It is one of the
recurring themes of twentieth-century thought and literature,
and particularly of those streams that have fed into hippie
culture. It found a persistent place in the literature of the
bohemian groups of the twenties and thirties. Moreover,
Camus's great novel, which took *The Outsider* for its title,
focused on two fundamental preoccupations of hippies: the
nature of anti-social, or rather non-social man, of man unto
himself; and the disturbing questions raised for the European
by the cultures of Africa and Asia. Most pertinently of all,
Hesse's *Steppenwolf*, a book written in 1927 but still often taken
to be something of a Bible for hippies, centres upon the outsider theme. It may be appropriate then to use the outsider
theme to express the nature and extent of that difference between 'hip' and 'straight', which we shall see our novitiates
traversing.

Most of us, of course, are to some degree insider and to some
degree outsider, depending on the point of reference of the
moment. Most of us are in some way or on some particular issue
rebels, identifying with particular subterranean values, even if
that identification finds little reflection in overt behaviour. With
most of us, moreover, fundamental attitudes and values fluctuate over time, and life remains always, in some ways, an
experiment: our situation is new in every moment and we are
always free to decide for the next moment what we are going
to do and what we are going to become. No social division by
consequence is ever absolute or entirely irrevocable.

That is not, however, the way in which it appears to the
kinds of outsiders with whom I am concerned. For them it is
not just a matter of shades of meaning, nor just a matter of
feeling oneself from time to time different in certain specific
particulars. It is not just a matter of commitment. It is a matter
of accepting a wholly different identity and career. It is that one
particular element of the individual's personality comes to
seem so important, so crucial and absorbing, that all the rest
has to be stabilised and consolidated around it. The one way in
which the individual differs from the majority—by being

persistently a thief, prostitute, drug-user or whatever—is taken to negate and disqualify all those ways in which he or she is similar. Just as the world sees all the acts done by someone who steals as the acts of a thief, so someone who steals is forced to see the world through the eyes of a thief and from the point of view of a thief. To the person who steals and sees nothing wrong in it, for example, it may then seem a quite sensible interpretation of the world that everyone else would also steal if only they had the courage. One arrives in such ways at a special and distinctive conception of human nature. When the individual is transformed and accepts some special identity, his perception of the world around him is transformed also. It is not too much to say that he comes to inhabit a different reality from that in which the conventional man dwells.

The member of the conventional majority, by contrast, is distinguished by his acceptance, however much his values and attitudes fluctuate, of that common perception of social reality on which the institutional means of a society depend for acceptance and effect. It involves a particular conception of man and of society—which dimensions of each are to be taken as real and which as false. It involves acceptance of a particular spatial and temporal grid by which alone interaction with others becomes mutually meaningful.[1] It involves a bedrock of shared opinion and behavioural routine. If such elements constrain and limit the individual's freedom in some respects, they are in other respects liberating: they at least provide that stable framework of controls that alone turns the random act into the meaningful experiment. All this the outsider leaves behind when he embarks on the process of gradual drift out of the conventional world and final transformation to a hippie identity which I shall describe.

IDENTITY AND INTERACTION PROCESSES

If the end result of the process of becoming a hippie was clear and distinct, the stages along the way were not. They are intimately bound up with the more usual processes of adolescence and youth. It was not easy to disentangle them: the former in many cases were primarily a distinctive texturing of the latter. Many of the features described in this chapter could, with only slight adjustment, have characterised more general processes of adolescence and maturity.

The particular problem was that the process of becoming a hippie (whether in youth or not) necessarily involved some kind of identity crisis. Such a crisis is common in adolescence and youth. This is characteristically the period at which the individual must, in Erikson's terms, make simultaneous commitment to physical intimacy, to decisive occupational choice, to energetic competition and psycho-social self-definition. It is in this sense that it is a crisis, a time of 'increased vulner- ability and heightened potential' (1968, p. 96). One way of looking at the matter would then be to conclude that being a hippie was a way of managing or resolving a very familiar kind of personal crisis.

Adolescence is not, of course, equally turbulent and troubled for all. The chances of feeling oneself the outsider and be- coming a hippie are therefore not randomly spread. A pro- portion of young people will always find themselves to be the children of their age, and in tune with its technological, economic and ideological trends. They are predominantly today those schooled in the sciences or with a commitment to particular technical competencies. By and large, hippies are not found among them. For such individuals, youth is not so deeply problematical, and indeed for them no real crisis of identity may occur. They discover in the historical culture into which they move a symmetry and congruence with their own values and skills. They move forward on the wave of the economic and technological trends of their times. Their identity is adequately defined by the roles the culture provides. They reinforce the culture they encounter and that culture validates them. They do not question it, and it does nothing to cause them to question themselves.

For those who finally accepted the hippie identity, how- ever, this identity crisis of adolescence is likely to have been particularly acute. Nick's experience had been characteristic:

Your ideas change so vastly in a short amount of time. You can ask yourself, who are you, but in six months the answer would be different. That's why to me the future is so pointless, in fact even thinking about it, because your personality can change completely, without your really knowing it. You sort of are in the present. You've got to live for the moment you're living in. Your character's changing every second, and your ideas are changing every second, so to look further ahead won't do you any good at all.

I've changed that much in two years. There's been the change of environment more than anything, and meeting different kinds of people. You're subject to violent changes. Finding your own self, finding your own way.

Those who've come out of it all, they look at you and laugh . . . and yet, you don't see your way out of it when you're in it.

Nick encapsulated here all the elements of the identity confusion of youth: career inhibition embodied in rejection of the future, the tendency to violent and unpredictable personal changes, a consciousness of their own identity problem and a certain intensity of concern about it. No doubt those experiencing identity confusion could seek out particular solutions to particular problems, but for most of them, most of the time, there was only the waiting.

The decisive choices that could commit the potential hippie to conventional society were many. The critical one, which Nick in the end could not take, and which laid him open to those various processes which ultimately make the hippie, was the matter of decisive occupational choice. Such a decision seemed to determine too many aspects of his life and identity.

There's two different kinds of work. There's working for someone or working for yourself.

The actual conforming work, which everybody seems to go through, I don't pretend to understand. I keep myself different, away from it. The more you get into it, the more you get involved in it and can't see out of it.

The same with the right society: you think, 'Well, it's wrong', and you start reading more and more about it until you're finally enveloped. You want to change it from the inside and you find yourself conforming to society: you didn't believe in the police force and you end up in the police force being the head of police or something.

If it's wrong I know I'm not attempting to put my boot in it. I know I'm on the outside.

Whether it is in the matter of work, attitudes to authority or whatever, the perennial divisions of conformity and rebellion are always presenting themselves, although in some cases they may appear clearly only in retrospect, and be the subject of infinite rationalisation. When confronted by these choices Nick and his fellows may not have positively chosen rebellion, as they so often claimed, but did at least fail to choose conformity. The rejection of commitments which the identity crisis of youth so often involves then entails at least their initial complicity in the process of action and reaction by which outsiders are finally made.

Among outsiders, more people think they make choices— even negative ones—than in fact do so, and such choices as are made are only one element in the process of interaction and mutual definition between outsiders and the representatives of the dominant social order which solidifies the division between them.[2] At some stage in the turbulent process of self-definition the seditious adolescent may see himself defined and rejected by the dominant society, who see 'only the drug-taking and the sex orgies'. He does not necessarily choose this but must react to it.

If you get a job or something, you're even more conforming to the system, and if you don't agree with it, where do you turn? So you see you kind of invent your own lifestyle—you think to yourself, society today, is it good for me or isn't it? And if you decide it isn't, you're lost, because they reject you for it, because you're different.

In some cases no doubt the rejection is less real than it is made to appear. Many young people, fearing the possibility of failure within society, may court their own exclusion, to transfer responsibility and relieve the possibility of such failure. Many do at some point *choose* to be outsiders, or choose to regard themselves as having become outsiders: and choose to consider that society so regards them. Most however, are left with little choice. Although, as we shall see, the outsider becomes the hippie in a conscious and nearly deliberate way, it is society that first of all makes the outsider.

Some, like Nick, willingly accepted the possibilities of the outsider's life, but others stumbled less willingly into it, and were the victims of exclusion and ban they neither sought nor understood, nor indeed had the personal resources to confront. Over this part of the process of becoming a hippie, most of those in the West End and many also of those in Ladbroke Grove had little control. In a real sense they were victims.

Ben's experience illuminates this. There is no way of verifying what he said. I quote it because he seemed transparently honest. Three incidents will do to clarify stages in the process. It began in his early youth, at school, when he was marked down to be the outsider by other children by reason of physical abnormality. They would single him out for assault with that unthinking savagery of which only the innocent are capable.

> I used to find that at school a lot of the very small people used to try to pick fights with me. And when I was 13 or 14 I was 6′1″, and I was thin. You might think that I'm thin now, but I was really thin then, and I'd just completely outgrown my strength. If I fell down I really couldn't get up again.

Already feeling an outsider in this way, his actions, through the pattern of time and other circumstance, came to confirm him in this role. The process of labelling implicit in the reactions of police and other agents of authority amplified his deviance, and drew more firmly in his eyes the line between himself and straight society. In this process, others conspired. He described an incident involving himself and a friend in Exmouth:

> Terry had a knife, it was just a normal knife but a fairly big one. He took it out to show a friend. I suppose you'd say we were pissed—but he's straight, he was the son of my boss. It was down the pub on pay day, and this copper came up.
> 'Hello, hello, what's this 'ere then?'
> Terry said, 'It's a knife.'
> 'Wise guy, eh?' And the copper started yapping on about an offensive weapon. We were standing down by the quay, over a bridge.
> 'That's an offensive weapon.'

Terry says, 'It's not, it's a knife.'

And the cop says, 'Well, how do I know, I think you'd better come along with me', and Terry—it was a foolish thing to do—but he threw it in the water and he got taken and he got charged. The papers made a big splash about it. They went just far enough: they exaggerated so much, but not enough to sue them. They said, 'Flick knife: Exmouth Flick Knife Man Charged with Offensive Weapon'. You know, it was just so funny! Terry was a flick knife man—and it was just so funny—and he wouldn't hurt a fly!

Such incidents progressively convinced him that he and his friends laboured under an exclusion not all of their own making.

We move on, then, in time and circumstance, to another incident which illustrates a further stage. Ben had meantime started using drugs and associating with West End hippies, and had undergone the sort of critical transformational process I shall describe in due course. He had finally become an outsider and a hippie, but he was not all or only that. Similar processes of labelling were still at work, however, now in the particular identity caricatures that straight society built of people like Ben.

In this case the issue was drugs. When challenged, Ben had to admit the act and accept the label. He was now among the lost. He described an incident at a factory where he briefly tried working.

There was one guy who reckoned all junkies should be shot. I nearly came to blows the first day I started there. He saw that tattoo [of a needle] and said 'What do you think of junkies?' And I said, 'They're O.K., if that's what they want to do'. And he said, 'I think they should all be shot', and we had a big argument about it.

Ben had to defend the junkies' cause because he did what they did, and in the process identified himself with them and acknowledged their label for himself. He was a junkie. He was a hippie. He was an outsider. The line was drawn. The identity once consolidated, he felt himself different. He was separated not only from those people who would shoot all junkies. He was separated also from the father, to whom—in good times at least—he had felt close:

> As soon as I met him, he bought me a pint, but I could feel vibes, bad vibrations. We just don't go down well together. He said he wouldn't be seen dead with me outside Charing Cross Station. I don't blame him though, because I had very long hair then. He had a bowler and a moustache, umbrella, pin-stripe suit. It didn't go very well. It clashes.

He was now separated also from the vast majority of young people. This majority included many who wore 'hip' clothes and espoused elements of the 'hip' life-style. He was separated from them because the processes we have been following had not reached the same culmination for them. The hip identity had not, as in Ben, been finally consolidated. They had not *become* hippies.

> The people I hate are the King's Road type. Chelsea. The Ravers. Weekend hippies. They wear what they call groovy clothes. They have long hair. But they're about as plastic as the cover of that tape recorder case. Maybe they have a pair of jeans like me—but when they first get outside you can still smell the moth-balls because they've had them hanging around all the year. They're hanging on the peg for 50 weeks of the year and they just take them out and wear them up town one night, smoke one joint and really think they're turned on, they've done it all.

Ben and his friends felt that there was something absolute and decisive about their tribal identity. Like Nick, they saw a clear line. Fashions in clothes and styles of living might be important but they were never enough. At some point or other the individual had to make an inductive leap, and *become* a hippie. Such an absolute division might be partly the product of the identity crisis of youth and the labelling processes of social interaction, but it could never be exclusively this. Normal interaction process accounts of the acquisition of deviant identity move from one stage to another by steps that are often scarcely perceptible, and often do not admit the possibility of there being any particular line over which the individual at

Transformation: Becoming a Hippie

some point or other passes, from *not being* a hippie to *being* one. Yet such a transition is how hippies saw the matter and explained themselves. Their own thoughts were important, moreover, because they were, as we shall see, the primary determinants of their subsequent behaviour.

TRANSFORMATION: THE MAKING OF THE HIPPIE

The people described in the previous chapter had in common that they recalled particularly decisive turning-points in the passage from not being a hippie to being one. Such moments were watersheds. Events before were seen to lead up to them and events afterwards flowed from them. While Ben, for example, graphically recalled the first occasion he injected drugs, and the critical physical and emotional experience it produced, for Maggie it was her first time in North Africa. Even Elaine recalled the sudden effect upon her of Beatlemania, and how it was critical in evoking interest in hippies.

I suggest, then, that some more immediate transformation was involved in becoming a hippie than just the particular involvements and upheavals of the adolescent moratorium and the interactional processes that could progressively absorb the individual in them. This deeper transformation was related to the search for, and encounter with, certain special modes of experience which I attempt to clarify at the end of this chapter. First, however, I must try to describe the pattern that such transformation normally followed.

An analysis of the kind of change that the adolescent becoming hippie undergoes, has been given by Berger and Luckmann (1967). Parts of my account are set in their framework and terminology. They were concerned with the common features of a wide range of possible transformations from one mode of experience and reality to another. They labelled them 'alternations' and defined a number of their characteristics, which we may here usefully make our starting-point. In the first place, the transformation is *subjectively apprehended as total*. Every element of the individual's personality is felt to be included and he does not entertain the possibility that the change might be reversed. That this is necessarily something of a misunderstanding does not affect the essential perception. Alternation,

83

argued Berger and Luckmann, requires *re-socialisation*, which, since no adolescent starts with his mind a *tabula rasa*, involves his coping *with a problem of dismantling, disintegrating the preceding nomic structure of subjective reality*. The important social condition for this disintegration is the availability of an effective *plausibility structure, a social base serving as the 'laboratory' of transformation*. This is typically mediated by strong affective ties with certain significant others, which recall the dependent ties of childhood, and with whom there is an intense concentration of significant interaction. Essentially the whole experience is similar to religious conversion.

How far may such an analysis fit entry into the hip world? To examine this I turn from settled members of hippie communities to several young people new to contact with them. Let us begin with Nick's description of his transformation.

I dropped out of art college after about a year. The course was bad in the fact that you had to cover everything virtually that there was, and you couldn't specialise in anything at all that you wanted to do.

I went to the art college with the idea that I'd be a sort of Picasso, you know what I mean, another Gauguin. You think, yeh, I'm good at art, so you don't make any fuss about it, you say, 'I'm good', and you sort of leave it there. It's very much a sort of ego thing.

But art college is a peculiar place where they try and break down everything you put up yourself—this is just ideas about art, first of all. But it's not only art, because if you're that much interested in art, art's part of your personality anyway. So, you know, for me, it just became one big revolt thing. I was doing my thing all the time, and of course they didn't like it. I spent most of my time doing what I wanted to and of course the write-up things and reports were really bad. I enjoyed it because I had the chance to do what I really wanted to.

Most of the time I was into a sort of contemporary way of illustration. Psychedelic stuff, not these sort of drastic posters you see, a sort of natural thing, growing art-form. But they didn't understand that.

Things like this, they change completely the way you

think, because you've got a certain number of tutors and they all sort of want you to end up being one of them—the way they work and the way they feel about things. This is very restricting, especially for an art college. After a while they kind of accepted that I was so much into my own thing that I didn't want to change the way I was working. They said, right he's doing what he wants to do, and they all thought he's stupid and said he'd change his ideas in a few years. But I think I learned a lot more from doing it my way than I would have doing it as they told me to do it.

Since I left college I've just been trying to get this commune together. At college there was a group of seven of us, and the idea of a commune grew on us. There was a friendship there among people that you don't find in ordinary people. I've been friends with ordinary people and it sort of lacks sincerity and the sort of togetherness of these friendships. And you get the best ideas from people you really know.

Before we went to college we were all sort of normal people, but we started growing long hair and blossoming out. And that's sort of stuck so far.

We see here the critical social conditions for transformation. Art college acted as a forcing house of personal change, dismantling and disintegrating the structure of concepts and values in which he felt not only his art but also his personality consisted. The young person's identity and self-esteem are in some measure inevitably buffeted and called into question by the competitive individualism encountered in college or in the world of work. In any circumstances they were liable to cause stress after the relatively comfortable and cosy particularism of family and school. In the special conditions of an art college this stress was so exacerbated that it came to be seen as an attempt to break down his structure of reality. That he could, almost certainly incorrectly, view this process as deliberate, indeed almost conspiratorial, at least testifies to the extent to which he felt his former self was undermined by it.

Like many people in the course of identity crises, Nick was at this time subversively individualistic, and the new reality subsequently consolidated was seen as something intensely personal. Even here, however, we see the critical mediating-role of significant others. The particularly deep relationships he entered while his old 'normal' self was disintegrating became the centre of a new identity. The commune, which had by this time become his single and total preoccupation, precisely expressed this wish that all elements of his new life should derive from and be consolidated around these relationships.

What was particularly important about the relationships mediating his transformation was not just their special content of feeling, but also that they had what might in a way be defined as an intellectual content: as Nick dimly perceived, it was from these close relationships that he got his best ideas. It may not be straining interpretation too far to suggest that, like the special experience of himself through art that first marked transformation, they were special because they were felt as experiences both of mind and feeling. In some measure Nick was bearing out the truth of Eliot's conclusion: 'It may be that men ripen best by experiences that are at once sensuous and intellectual' (Matthiessen, 1958, p. 14). In the end, however, other people only mediate transformation. That transformation is ultimately sustained by the new plausibility structure into which the individual moves. Significant others may be one part of that plausibility structure, but some conceptual framework is also required. This conceptual framework is provided by the hippie philosophy, and in the next chapter I shall examine Nick's perception of this and how it relates to the ideas of his old 'normal' self before its disintegration.

This then is the drama in which the detail of interaction process is enmeshed. How far was there for Nick a *moment* of transformation? There was certainly a critical point of change, and in retrospect it seemed almost to be tied to a moment in time: 'One particular piece of work I was doing—I became aware of it becoming incredibly real. That piece of work became important to me because it was opening me up. It was like a drug experience. I didn't realise I was experiencing the same sort of things I was experiencing in my work.'

Nick's story illustrates the normal process of transformation. The details might vary enormously, but the basic structure conventionally followed this pattern. In one way, however, a large proportion of hippies did diverge from it. Nick in a sense stumbled into the disintegration of his former self and stumbled equally into his new self. Though never as swift or decisive or real, it may at least have been as unexpected as Saul's conversion on the Road to Damascus. For many hippies, however, the loss of their former selves and the discovery of their new identity involved a long, deliberate and intense search. In this circumstance the final conversion and discovery were not surprisingly perceived in more heightened terms. John, a young Australian hippie, finally settled in London, not far from Nick. This account comes from a journal he kept for his own interest:

I was born in Tasmania, and spent the first twenty years of my life there. At some stage I became very interested in the world beyond my small island where nothing happened. Every day I would read in the local paper the events that took place in far-off places like England, and America, and even in Australia. I became fairly convinced that my local paper wasn't telling it as it was, especially when I became particularly interested in Indonesia and met some students from Indonesia.

About this time, too, echoes of Bob Dylan could be discerned, and a group called the Beatles began to overrun the world—but it was all happening over there—in America or England or Australia, and nothing continued to happen in Tasmania.

I just managed to fail my university entrance examination and found myself in a Bank amongst a lot of money, doing work which I knew I could not endure for long. After a couple of years I had rebelled to the extent that I owned my own car, and regularly got drunk and dragged around town looking for women and parties, with my friends, and always got into financial difficulties because I believed that I had to fix every dent I put in my car, which was my entire life.

But something inside was denied, and I couldn't find it in Tasmania. I caused a few rumbles in the Bank and got myself transferred. Thought this would solve it all, but decided that it wasn't much different from being back in

Tasmania, because I was still in the Bank. I resigned not long after that and went into a state administration, which wasn't much different from the Bank, except that there was more chance of getting something that I could reasonably expect to enjoy. It was becoming clear that it is hard to be in a job you want to do.

Lasted a year there altogether, during which time I came into brief contact with the International Hippie Convoy, black men, and made a friend of someone who had been in the drug scene for several years, all of which were new experiences.

I took a job with a company mining in an Aboriginal reserve. There I made friends with a group of Aborigines who were employed by the company. I did my best to learn as much as I could about them, and succeeded in convincing myself that these people have more to teach us than we have to teach them—about how to live.

In November 1969 I set off by plane from Australia to Indonesia. Before leaving I burned a large pile of exercise books in which I had recorded many of my experiences and thoughts over the preceding four or five years.

In Indonesia I discovered more than I had expected. Friendly, unspoiled people who seemed to live in perfect harmony. I was completely overwhelmed by their generosity and hospitality. They were the most happy, contented, uninhibited people I have ever seen.

For three months I travelled in Indonesia and the impression it made on me will never be erased. They leave me without any means of expressing the impression they made on me. Their entire nature seemed to be a complete contradiction to everything wrong with my own country and presumably the Western World.

Incidentally I was introduced to the international convention of hashish smoking, and met more of the International Head Convoy.

Eventually I was in Singapore when there happened what works out to be a culmination of all previous experiences. With the vivid memory of Indonesia impressed on my brain, the oriental surroundings of Singapore celebrating the Chinese New Year, and abundance of good grass and groovy people, it had to happen.

All of a sudden I was exposed to myself and at last I knew who I was. I remember telling my friend that I had found myself and I was no longer searching for anything.

Quest over, happiness achieved, self-confidence regained. What to do? Nothing I can't do. Nothing stopping me doing what I want. What do I want?

Because of my Indonesian student friends, because of my Aboriginal friends, because of the beautiful representatives of the hippie movement I had met, because of Indonesia—all I wanted was to do my best to make sure all these people are free and able to be themselves and don't ever get forced into the horrifying mould of what is called Western Civilisation of all things. I decided that all that was wanted was peace. Complete peace and complete freedom for everybody in the world. There were no barriers to be overcome, and nothing was standing in the way. All I had to do was get myself in a position in which I could address the world, tell my story, relate it to each individual's experience, and we would have peace. All it takes is for everybody in the world to have an Instant Karma and there will be peace, and every technological advancement would be directed towards healing the scars man has made across the face of the earth and across the faces of his fellow men.

The time for heaven to happen is here. There is not one person on earth who cannot be changed by the same forces that changed me from the half man I was into the whole man I find myself to be.

John provides the classic account of youth in crisis—the inner pressure to turn either towards empty violence and display or progressive self-destruction. The only alternative lies in escape from the dominant social order, whose civilised routines and deceptive ambiguities have become oppressive. There then begins that seeking after the self which seems a recurrent characteristic of youthful rebellion.

John's journey began out of a sense of deprivation and disappointment after failing to get into university, like Nick's discovery at art college that he was not a Picasso or Gauguin. Gradually his focal concern became, characteristically, the issue of the primitive and the civilised, the artificial and the natural:

> I was interested in Aborigines. In the government I was in the wrong job. I was never in contact with the Aborigines. I would occasionally see one walking down the office corridor, but that was all. I was interested to know from my Aborigine friends how the encroachment of Western civilisation had affected him, and how it affects me. I found he thought pretty much as I thought, which was nice. Made me think maybe I am right and civilisation wrong.

The basic pattern, too, was the one already described: the turbulent searching of the adolescent moratorium, total breakdown of personality and values by 'the impression that will never be erased' of Indonesia, followed by discovery of a new self in the experience in Singapore. That this was a special kind of peak experience the description leaves no doubt. Present again was that agitation of the mind ('Indonesia impressed upon my brain') in intimate harmony with that of the senses ('the oriental surroundings of Singapore celebrating the Chinese New Year') producing an experience of wholeness and identity: John being 'exposed to himself'.

My final example of the transformation which is the key event in the process of becoming a hippie, has in its structure a fundamental similarity to Nick's and John's. Like theirs, Jeremy's transformation began with disappointment. After failing to get into Cambridge he went from his public school to an American university to read business studies. It was at the beginning of the troubles on the campuses of America, but Jeremy did not expect that these would impinge much upon him.

> I went to the university with the assumption that I was not going to make many friends, that I would just introvert, and get very involved in my studies. Previously I was very conservative in outlook, extremely, and I was aware of it. I cultivated it. My manner of education, dress, hair, social activities was very conservative.
>
> What changed me was circumstances and how I reacted to them; and becoming a leader, politically, on the campus.

Then I was creating the circumstances. I enjoyed it, I got a great kick out of leading it.

I was totally dissatisfied with conditions at the university. Among other things, I felt I had had more freedom at school. But I enjoyed the time immensely more than my last year at school, which was academically a series of disappointments. There was no comparison. It was more a contrast with my whole English way of life rather than my last year at school. I felt that then as well.

What was particularly attractive about it? Well, I suppose it was the second time I became a true believer. After being born and brought up in the same mould all the way, that all changed into a concern for a great number of things, and a knowledge about so many things, and I enjoyed that. All the winter term I used to stay up till two just listening and talking.

And the other thing is, retrospectively, I became a great believer in widening your range of experience, widening your frame of reference the whole time, so that you can accept something for itself. It was possible for someone like me—who left England ex-Public School and Royal Enclosure at Ascot—to go right across the culture and class spectrum and down, filling in all the squares on the way.

Transformation consisted here in the breaking down of Jeremy's original conceptual and value structure, and in the new sense of life and mission deriving from the stimulation and excitement of campus political leadership. The plausibility must have derived in part at least from suddenly finding others willing to follow his new ideas and beliefs, and thus give them vicarious confirmation.

The new structure was again mediated in a most critical way by significant others. What was important to Jeremy, and what had indelibly marked him, was the sharing of critical experience. There is a sense in which the importance and intensity of all *critical* experience derives from the presence in a single movement, and to unusual degree, of both intellectual and sensuous dimensions. In retrospect Jeremy seemed to have had to go half across the world for this kind of critical experience.

If you've been with your back against the wall with people and you put implicit trust in them, then there's always afterwards that certain bond. If you are questioned by the police and if you could have said one thing that could put people in jail for five or ten years and you didn't, because they didn't; and if you've been in a demonstration where heads are getting cracked together, and you've got out of it together, and at the same time not flinched at any time, then a tremendous feeling of trust builds up. You never get the opportunity to test that in England.

To make people aware, is to have some of the same sort of experiences. In England there's far more of an element of choice and of avoidance of an issue and what you get involved in. In America the issue's there and people can see how you react to it. In England you need never get near an issue, so that sort of evaluation need never occur.

Jeremy was forced to face the issue. In the intensified experience involved in confronting this crisis, he discovered a new sense of identity. It led him to become a hippie of a sort. It was in many ways like the route our other informants took to becoming hippies, most of all in that it was felt as absolute. There was no going back.

THE NATURE OF TRANSFORMATION

These accounts raise several questions. What is the range of possible 'agencies' of transformation: is it just a matter of special experiences such as art college and contact with non-Western peoples, or can more common experiences act in the same way? Are these three accounts extreme and special cases, or will the majority of hippies make reference to some such experience? What are the pre-conditions for conversion: why, for example, did art college affect Nick but not others in the way it did? Is the transformation experienced as real at the time, or is such an explanation just rationalisation after the event? Finally, if such transformation is real, what endows it with compelling effects?

The agencies of transformation I have chosen to follow in

this chapter were certainly among the less obvious available. The experience of art college, contact with non-Western peoples, or campus rebellion, could frequently be critical points in the moral careers of the adolescent as he moved from the dominant social order to immersion in the 'hip scene', but it was clear that in this role they were much less prevalent than, for example, drugs and pop music. I shall deal with these influences separately in a later chapter because of their particular and pervasive significance. Overall, however, it appeared that a wide range of experiences could have a transformational role, even though the basic developmental pattern was similar. The two propositions about it to which the interviewing lent support were, first, that drugs and music were the typical agents, because they were so prevalent and communicable; and second, although in their form the range of possible agents is in principle unlimited, in practice certain particular themes recurred: the choice of examples reflects my belief that certain kinds of culture-contact and of aesthetic activity were particularly common as agents and precipitants of transformation.

Do all hippies undergo such a transformation? Since I avoided placing any particular definitional limits to what was to be regarded as a hippie, it is difficult to say. I was concerned with what was common to a necessarily ill-defined range of individuals, but of these it can be said that the majority claimed such an experience. There were of course exceptions. Elaine was the obvious one. Helen and Jason were others, but in a sense they were exceptions that proved the rule, because unlike the others they were born to a bohemian setting. Otherwise, most of those met in the previous chapter, and more particularly those described in the subsequent sections on drugs and music, identified some critical experience which conformed to this pattern. The examples quoted in this and subsequent chapters are more dramatic than the average, but it is only in this that they are unrepresentative.

Obviously not everyone who tried drugs, or became a devotee of certain sorts of music, or visited Indonesia or Afghanistan, or became involved in campus politics, underwent transformation. It was necessary, as I said, that the individual be ready and the moment auspicious. This depended on many things. It demanded the various factors that Berger and Luckmann identified. It demanded also that the individual involved be already something of an outsider, and already caught up in some of the interactional processes of exclusion and ban. It normally demanded also that the individual feel not some generalised sense of discontent, but some more immediate disappointment. All these elements made the individual vulnerable to the sort of commitments and behaviour which characterised my informants and which followed from transformation.

The subsequent question, about the validity and reliability of the accounts of transformation, is more fundamental, and more difficult to answer. One thing can be said confidently: it does not matter whether the particular transformational experience was, objectively viewed, of some transcendent character. In the evaluation of such experience subjective judgment is absolute. 'Objective' criteria (were they possible) would have little relevance. What is important is what the individual himself believes, for it is upon this that he acts.

The more substantial issue is whether the experience of transformation was really seen at the time it happened, or only interpreted in this way some time afterwards. This question is unanswerable. I suspect it is probably true that the experience seemed more dramatic in retrospect. The logic of my argument requires only, however, that there should have been a moment of commitment, and this I think there was in all cases. In a sense such commitment requires prior transformation, and, to some extent, that the actors be conscious of the transformation. To this extent, I believe that the accounts may be credited.

The key point in the argument, however, has been the implication that transformation, whatever form it took, always involved some qualitatively different mode of experience. In the longer run the individual would only believe himself a special person, and behave as one, if he in some sense felt himself to be one. In summarising what such a mode of experience might involve, my account must be very tentative.

Three characteristics are obvious: it was certainly in some sense intensified experience, and it also appeared to have, in adolescence in particular, some special relationship to growth. It was also, to quite an unusual degree, an acute identity experience. Identity has been a persistent issue in the accounts I have discussed. John's transformation was marked by a quite sudden feeling of being 'exposed to himself', and Nick's by a particular piece of art which he sensed was 'opening him up'. Such acute identity experiences are of course not uncommon, and certainly not confined to transformation. They are perhaps no more than what Mrs Adams felt at certain special moments in her leisure, when she felt 'taken out of herself'. It appears, however, that the individual feels, to a particularly marked degree, his sense of identity involved in transformational experiences.

Such characteristics may follow from the recurrent dimensions of the experience. Invariably the object, whether it was a painting, some newly-encountered culture, a particular drug experience, or whatever, was attended to with a total absorption. In common with Maslow's interpretation of peak experiences (1968), the object was also experienced as a whole, detached from usefulness, expediency and purpose, and about it there was 'a very characteristic disorientation in time and space'. The experience was transcendent because of this total personal absorption and because of the detachment it involved from those social roles and routines among which individual identity and experience is normally divided.

It may derive, however, from the more subtle fact that identity implies unity, and of all the divisions that the individual can feel in his experience and sense of self the most critical is that which may separate sensuous and intellectual experience. Part of the specialness of transformation, and of all acute identity experiences, may be the momentary feeling of transcending this separation. A shared characteristic of almost all those aspects of an advanced industrial society which the hippie most rejected was that they embodied in a particularly marked degree such separation of the intellectual and sensuous. This was most obviously true of routines and the planning of time and the saving of money, and, at its most general level, of the special separation of work and leisure and the particular modes of experience which each allowed.

Such an interpretation may be strengthened by later chapters, for it may appear that the attempt to transcend this separation marked not only the experience of transformation but broad areas of hippie culture and values. Two disconnected remarks about rock music and drugs, integral parts of this culture may presage my argument on this point. The first point is made by a recent history of rock and roll music, which described its importance as follows:[3]

> What rock 'n' roll has done for us won't leave us. Faced with the bleakness of social and political life in America, we will return again and again to rock 'n' roll, as a place of creativity and renewal, to return from it with a strange, media-enforced consciousness increasingly a part of our thinking and our emotions, two elements of life that we will less and less trouble to separate.

Second, what in general young people consider the value of drugs is their capacity to heighten and relate intellectual and sensuous appreciation. The dimensions along which one characteristically appreciates each become confounded: shapes and colours change, the inanimate comes alive, conventional categories of experience and appreciation are confounded. It is in this sense that I suggest that what most hippies sought, in most areas of their life, was to transcend the separation of thought and feeling. They did not of course do this in any conscious or deliberate way. It was simply that this mode of experience, for most of them first encountered in transformation, left such a deep imprint on their sense of what it was to be alive that they were thereafter subconsciously drawn to re-enact it.

The reader may here be puzzled by my argument. He may be puzzled, first of all, that I designate this mode of experience special, since normal conceptions of healthy behaviour usually emphasise some balancing of the intellectual and sensuous. Most people, moreover, find something repellent about an excessive preoccupation with either one or other. This does not contradict my argument, for I am not referring to some *balancing* of these kinds of experience—with which each of us is all the time involved—but rather to their fusion, which is a quite different matter.

He may be puzzled secondly because an argument about the separation and fusion of intellectual and sensuous experience inevitably involves difficult metaphysical assumptions. Hippies would not, however, be the first group of people whose leitmotif was found here. He would join, at very least, the poets and the madmen, much no doubt to his satisfaction. It was only through this that Eliot could explain (1932, pp. 287-8) changes in poetic form over the last few centuries:

> Something had happened to the mind of England between the time of Donne or Lord Herbert of Cherbury and the time of Tennyson and Browning: it is the difference between the intellectual poet and the reflective poet. Tennyson and Browning are poets, and they think; but they do not feel their thought as immediately as the odour of a rose. A thought to Donne was an experience; it modified his sensibility . . .
>
> We may express the difference by the following theory: the poets of the Seventeenth Century . . . possessed a mechanism of sensibility which could devour any kind of experience . . . In the Seventeenth Century a dissociation of sensibility set in, from which we have never recovered.

And when Michel Foucault came to write the history of insanity (1967, p. 88), he saw madness as a sort of derivative of passion, which was itself to be located at the meeting ground of body and soul:

> If it is true that there exists a realm, in the relations of soul and body, where cause and effect, determinism and expression, still intersect in a web so dense that they actually form only one and the same movement which cannot be dissociated except after the fact; if it is true that prior to the violence of the body and the vivacity of the soul, prior to the softening of the fibres and the relaxation of the mind, there are qualitative, as yet unshared kinds of *a priori* which subsequently impose the same values on the organic and on the spiritual, then we see that there can be diseases such as madness which are from the start diseases of the body *and* of the soul, maladies in which the affection of the brain is of the same quality, of the same origin, of the same nature, finally, as the affection of the soul.
>
> The possibility of madness is therefore implicit in the very phenomenon of passion.

IV

THE WISDOM OF EXCESS

In becoming a hippie the experience of transformation was critical. The quirks and idiosyncrasies that first make the outsider, the minor habits of speech and dress that evoke the label 'hippie', and the pressures of social interaction that create and confirm deviant identity, in the end all had only supporting roles for the people in this book. The crucial element was always some intensified experience which in some sense made the individual see himself and the world in a different way, and which could thus ground a belief that he had become a different person. The people described in the previous chapters felt such transformation as a new beginning, and saw themselves embarking in a wholly new direction. Where, then, did it lead?

This is the subject of this and the following chapter. They are concerned with the shared patterns of thought and behaviour which distinguished individuals come by very different paths to a common beginning. In this chapter the main concern is with perceptions, attitudes and values, and the discussion will focus on two issues: first, their source; and second, their coherence and consistency. These two questions will, however, become one, because it will become clear that most of the coherence the beliefs and values possess derives from their common origin in the process of becoming a hippie: the novitiate hippie *grows into* hippie philosophy just because it is fundamentally an interpretation of transformational experience, and the only philosophy congruent with it. Such a contention risks becoming platitudinous. In anyone's life there is always an attempt to impose on fragmented impressions, experiences and actions a measure of form and coherence: a person's present is largely an interpretation of his past. Like everyone else, the hippie must continually reinterpret the world, and can do this only in terms of his own developing experience.

What may justify my particular argument is the level at which I pitch it. I try to move from the more obvious links to suggest a congruence, at a structural level, between the experience of transformation and the philosophy which is subsequently espoused. To do this I revert, to begin with, to Nick, our original guide. He was typical in the process by which he became a hippie, and typical also in the philosophy he then followed. The reader will see that his philosophy drew heavily upon that basic stock of beliefs which is generally found underlying a bohemian way of life and which was outlined in the Introduction. This, however, provided no more than a starting-point and frame of reference. The reader will see that the central fact was the complex relationship of beliefs and values to individual experience.

THE PRISONS OF THE MIND

The conventional man's implied theory of society generally rests on those things that ensure its capacity for survival. For outsiders like Nick and his friends the focus is rather on the potential for liberation, and in particular on the key to it, the differing possibilities of knowledge inside society and outside it. It is with this then that we begin. My informants' theory of society had to be a theory of liberation, but in its particular form and content it derived directly from the personal experience of liberation which transformation had given.

The first element was a particular perceptual image of society. This showed the effects of the process of disintegration in the first stage of transformation which had undermined the credibility of the dominant social order and emptied its concepts and values of meaning. This initial perception was rapidly built into an article of faith: 'society' became 'system', a network of formal and empty categories which obscured 'true reality' and restricted the individual's potential for experience:

> People can't see true reality. They're living in a kind of prison, and because they've grown up in this prison they can't think further than it.
>
> This is what a lot of society is today—a big prison. Maybe people don't want to get out. All the time though, there is a window, even if the rest is brick wall: but some

people have been in the prison so many years they sort of prefer to be there.

It's a sort of flexible prison. It's like one that's capable of being expanded, and that can always be made to look nicer. But it's still not wholly outside, because outside there's no restriction at all.

As soon as you see true reality, you can understand that this is what society is like. You can understand what makes society tick.

The bricks in the wall are so many ties and restrictions there is in everything, restrictions involved in subjection to government, in just everything outside the ordinary human personality. Everything's been constructed around it to make life better, or he thinks he's making it better just because he's making it more understandable. He's putting it into boxes—things which he doesn't understand—just so he can understand them more, but now people are beginning to wonder whether it was worth putting them into boxes in the first place.

The relationship between perceiving individual and blind society here mirrored and grew from Nick's own outsider status. The image of prison and window reflected the sudden sense of discovery and illumination of the peak experience, just as did reference to the sudden flash of understanding. This general breakdown of belief in conventional social categories was reflected in particular concepts, such as those of work and leisure, and of the work role.

For me there's no division into work and leisure. I'd hate to call myself an artist—I just draw. It's like a flower, growing all the time; you sort of blossom out and then you die. Or you find something else, maybe, or you just die. Enjoy it as it is at the moment.

It was also reflected in his conception of time and his attitude to planning and to possessions.[1] In the Introduction I suggested that these were widely considered key elements in the restriction of experience, and sources of the particular type of sensibility against which hippies revolted. The hippies' rejection of them, however, had not been built out of detached social criticism, but had an important experiential base. In Nick's case it grew out of the attempt to describe his time 'on the road' during the period of transformation, when the conventional categories of time and activity broke down, and when for once all the disparate elements of sense and activity came to seem just a single experience.

It's stupid planning for the future. You live for the moment, surely. No matter how much you plan ahead, you're still living for the moment, and you can't deny the fact. It all depends how you use it.

I never do things like save. I suppose I'm not particularly worried about money. To me money's stupid, it's not worth bothering about. The only way to stop bothering about it is to have none at all—it makes you sort of respond more to your own sort of ideas and things.

When you have got money, you tend to start planning things, whereas without money, you tend to think just of the next day. I was on the road a bit last summer, and I didn't think ahead at all, not at all, because it's really restricting. Perhaps when the next concert is coming up—that's all, and well, where you can get a packet of fags, and that's as far as you go. And in the meantime, things just build up and you tended to think of the whole thing as one experience, rather than sort of anything planned—more a natural thing.

I suppose I'm not very aware of time. I don't wear a watch. I don't believe in time at all. Because that is another thing that's so obvious. It's classification of an abstract thing, which is the ultimate in restriction. It's all very nice and convenient—you know, people say 'I've got to go out at 3 o'clock'—you can sort of rely on them. And we made all this for ourselves, sort of constructed it. But the point is that there are so many things that we take for granted. We don't realise what life is around us.

His perceptions of the social order and of time and money were important in themselves. I shall pursue their various implications in due course. At this stage it is more important to see that they were part of a wider vision of the nature of life which was equally related to the peak experiences of transformation. Nick was characteristic of hippies in his conception of what it was to be human. For him it resided above all in the possibility of a mental life that was spontaneous and intuitive, elevating the flash of insight above the routine patterns of rational deductive thought. For Nick that flash of insight had its paradigm in the one particular painting which, as we saw in the previous chapter, for him had stood for his whole transformation. The key, he concluded, was detabulation, that same rejection of linear structures that we have already seen expressed in his perception of the social reality and in his rejection of planning and money.

> I don't think that understanding comes from knowledge or facts. I don't think it does. You get to a level where people are trying to explain too many things. They can't really. It's like a comedy show.
>
> What's important is a kind of subconscious way of being able to understand things without consciously evaluating them. And this is an attitude of mind. It's what life is about. I can't really explain it: there's nothing sort of logical about it. It's just there, the same as you're a person. It's more a sort of instinctive thing. It's rare that I talk about things, sort of criticise things. I feel I've got this understanding—that I understand what life's about—and the rest of it doesn't matter.

The possibility of a knowledge derived by intuitive understanding paralleled the possibility of a spontaneous existence that was a response to natural stimuli rather than constrained by pre-ordained routines. Together they represented a rejection of the traditional conception of Western man, built as it is on the image of the rational mind discovering itself by subjecting the disorder of nature to utilitarian purpose. This, traditionally, was the way Western man discovered himself. Now, for the hippies, the journey to the self had to be inward:

> People get into this highly mechanised way of life—they just respond to the constructed things around them that are making the world the way it is at the moment. I know it sounds ridiculous—and yet on the one side you've got this highly mechanised life—and on the other side he's still

man, as he always was. And what's the good of having a
highly mechanised life, it doesn't suit us anyway—we're
still animals whether we've got cars that do 190 mph or
not.

It's all so pointless. To me, man's trying to prove
something to himself by his driving powers, just trying
to prove himself, trying to find himself the mechanical
way rather than looking into himself to find himself.

He's not going to do it by mechanical aids. They're no
answer to it—it will just get more and more complex, and
then he will be totally lost, cut off from his own reality.

His own reality is a quality everyone possesses, it's just
being human. You can't define it, it's something that you
know, the same as you recognise anyone that's the same
as you—someone you instantly recognise in the street,
something you can't describe, yet underneath it all, somewhere, there's this total experience which can't be dissolved.

The sense of suspension and waiting common to the adolescent moratorium often predisposes youth to commitment to
millennial causes, as one solution to their problem. This possibility was heightened for the hippies by the collapse of formal
time structure, by the 'living for the day' which they espoused
and indeed by the near rejection of the future as a category
that had any meaning. Just as John proclaimed 'the time for
heaven to happen is here', so Nick now added a dynamic
element to the theory of life he based on his images of natural
and constructed worlds. A projection of his own experience
led to the conclusion that the apocalypse was at hand: the
transformation he himself went through would be re-enacted on
cosmic scale, and would finally put an end to history and to
logic. John's tentative conclusion, that there was no one on
earth who could not be changed by the same forces that changed
him, was formalised by Nick into a theory of the inevitable
and impending transformation of all mankind.

We've been through a stage in human life. Since it started
off it's got more complex on one side and we've remained
the same on the other side. It's getting so complex that
another way of life becomes so obvious. People are
getting to realise what society's put them on to and every-

body's going to change at the same time. For man the only thing can be total advancement to his ultimate self. The man-made part of life, the creation of man, is getting out of hand. It's getting to the point where he doesn't understand what he's creating.

When you look at life, at animals and things, you see they've got a kind of society that works. When you think of something as diminutive as an ant, their society works. To me that's instinctive. And humans have got this—only they're sort of constructing something that's deformed, they're sort of growing it wrongly.

From one person to another these basic attitudes and values varied in detail—and important detail—but the same fundamental pattern of ideas recurred. The philosophy was intimately bound up with the process of transformation. To some extent, indeed, it was a rationalisation of transformation after the event, an attempt to describe and explain its essential character. This becomes more apparent when we turn from the general perception of society and social change to some of the more precise questions it raises, the perception and evaluation of time, material possessions, personal relationships, and most critically, the problem of action.

THE EXPERIENCE OF THE MOMENT

Time, protested Nick, is stupid: the ultimate in restriction, a classification of an abstract thing. Few members of conventional society would say that. For them it has a firm and reliable existence in two particular respects. It exists, to begin with, in the general acceptance of that particular pattern of time notation which is embodied in timetables and routines. It is often this scheduling and synchronisation of social activity that gives meaning: a particular action is performed by people at a particular 'moment' in a sequence of such moments, and it may be part of the definition of such activity that it should be performed at that moment.

'Time' also gains reality, however, by the way this acceptance is integrated in the individual's experience—both in his perception of the world and in his behaviour within it. People may be sensitive in different degrees to the 'passing' of time. At one extreme life may represent the subordination of the present moment to the future; each activity may be part of a carefully articulated sequence extending far into the future, each act and each moment deliberately and purposefully related to each other. At the other extreme life may be an apparently unstructured exuberance, a 'living for the moment'. In this case, each action is built, each moment is measured, not by the future but by the past. Whereas in the first case the future is the criterion, and the passing of time relatively unimportant, in the latter the passing of time assumes a different and greater importance. Talk to someone who subordinates the present to the future and he will tell you about what he is planning. Talk to a person who 'lives for the moment' and he will tell you about the 'good scenes' he has had in the past.

There is extensive evidence that people in different social situations perceive and evaluate time in such different ways. One study has suggested that children of different social classes differ in their awareness of time; another that a particular 'over-evaluation of time' may result from parental dominance. It has been suggested indeed that different attitudes to time may parallel, or at least be linked with, pattern of aesthetic choice, and that they may be closely linked also to the individual's degree of 'achievement motivation'. A study of people confined for long periods to hospital has suggested they may come to experience and evaluate time in a manner different from those in the everyday world outside.[2] In different kinds of social situation, 'social time' may assume different form and importance and the individual may sense and respond to it in quite different ways.

Hippies, however, were an extreme case. They were detached at almost every point from the normal time schedules and routines of the dominant society. In part this derived from the traditional bohemian rejection of such routines, which Ben articulated and which other informants endorsed equally strongly. In part it was the inevitable consequence of doing the things they wished to do and living the way they wished to live. If one wanted to sit late into the night listening to music; or if one wanted to be the noctambulist, as had all the Romantic and bohemian groups before the hippies, and to experience the particular sensation of mind and body that darkness might evoke, then there was no possibility of joining the 8.30 a.m. march to work the next day. As the weeks passed the everyday routines implicitly rejected by the hippie life-style were explicitly rejected in evolving attitudes and values.

Their rejection of everyday routines by word and deed was in itself less important than the fact that in the process they acquired a different conception and experience of time of their own. In some ways this was inevitable. The conventional person articulates himself, gains a knowledge of himself and a sense of his own identity, by the behavioural routines into which he is locked. He is a father because he arrives home each evening in time to say goodnight to his children, a husband because he helps his wife with the washing-up, a worker because he leaves home for the office the next morning. All the actions are tied into regularly repeated cycles. The nature of the activity is important for defining one's sense of self, but the fact of its regular repetition contributes directly to identity definition. The experience of time and the sense of the self are always connected, either the one causing the other or both deriving from a common source.

The hippie's rejection of everyday routines, and of the self-definition they provided, was made possible by occasional intensified experiences which not only had the appearance of transcending time but also provided a particularly heightened sense of the self. By such experiences the individual outside the dominant social order was saved from disintegration, and a sense of self of a special kind was established. This was the nature of the original experience of transformation, and, as we shall see in the next chapter, its periodic renewal and re-enactment at pop festivals and similar rituals. It was a large element in the significance of drugs, their capacity seemingly to take the individual 'outside time', even if only by 'being lazy and enjoying it', by making the individual feel his whole body and by making the mind peculiarly responsive to and at one with the body. It was also a large element in the appeal of pop music, and certainly linked to what many 'Underground' groups explicitly sought in the attempt to shock their audiences out of their inhibitions. The important implication is that, just because such critical experiences do produce a heightened sense of the self, social routines can be rejected, and a more disordered and chaotic life pursued in the days, weeks or even months between each renewal of the experience.

This makes it possible to see the significance of other hippie attitudes and behaviour. The rejection of the 'planning' of time and forward scheduling of activity becomes inevitable. They could necessarily play little part in a life which was dominated by the possibility of transcendent experiences which were by their nature largely spontaneous and unpredictable. Moreover they were the kind of experiences which by their apparent 'timelessness' undermined the belief in planning and the capacity for it. This was particularly the case with those experiences, such as drug-induced experiences, which could in fact extend for a long time, and thus directly undermined any normal existence. It is true that all the people we have met may have had in common this incapacity or unwillingness to plan even before becoming hippies, those in the West End to a particularly marked degree. While it is difficult to reconstruct this aspect of their personal histories, most of them appear originally to have found it difficult to plan because of some personal idiosyncrasy which excluded them from the conventional routines of their contemporaries, and thus deprived them of the social foundation and framework for the planning of their lives, such as Sue's lesbianism, or Ben's precocity. Some initial discordance may generally have been there, but this was then accentuated by the patterns of living into which the initial discordance helped to lead them. Hippies were, by and large, people who would probably have found it more than usually difficult to plan, even were they living a conventional life, but the hippie life finally undermined the possibility there was. An even greater obstacle was the fact already implied, that their mental life was absorbed in concentration upon critical events in the past, to which their thoughts as well as their feelings continually returned.

A related element is the millennialism which was their characteristic mode of perception of the future. We saw Nick, John and David all anticipating the imminent transformation of the world and the end of history, and we shall see others in subsequent chapters. Millennial creed shave generally developed among outsiders, the unemployed and unemployables on the margins of society (Cohn, 1967). In part it is a consequence of their predicament. It allows them the comfort of belief in an impending day of judgment when the injustices they bear will be ended and their oppressors chastised. It also reflects, however, the fact that as outsiders, without the support which the routines and roles of the dominant social order provide, they find it particularly difficult to manage time and plan activity. This in its turn means that they find untenable the conventional conception of the future as an orderly trajectory of activity capable of indefinite extension. Routine sequences of activity provide evidence of the passing of time and events, and it is only upon such evidence that the possibility of the future is constructed. Excluded from meaningful routines, the individual is deprived of the conventional image of the future. From where is his alternative to the future, the conception of a millennium or apocalypse, derived? The probable answer is those occasional, intense and 'timeless' experiences—original transformation and subsequent re-enactment—which come upon the outsider, or which he is able to induce in himself. Apocalypse and millennial transformations are the externalisations of inner experience, the projection onto the world of the personal experience of transformation. The essential structure and meaning is the same. Among the informants John almost explicitly indicated such a link. It is the vision of Instant Karma: 'The time for heaven to happen is here. There is not one person on earth who cannot be changed by the same forces that change me.'

THE EXPERIENCE OF THINGS

An old saying, that time is money, is often taken to express the core of the protestant ethic. Between the conventional concepts of time and possessions there is an obvious link: it is the essence of the proprietary relationship that it endures over time. In a sense the individual's possessions are absorbed into his self, or at least they become extensions of it. In societies such as our own, moreover, possessions often denote status. For both reasons possessions are a key influence on personal identity. The hippie rejected this web of relationships. He rejected the linkage between property and status, partly, of course, because of a familiar distrust of the notion of social status. More significant, however, was his rejection of the relationship between property and identity. If hippie behaviour was motivated and sustained by a search for a specially heightened sense of the self, the rejection of property and possessions had to follow almost automatically, just because these diverted attention outwards to the material world rather than inwards where alone, the hippie believed, any intense sense of the self could be discovered.

We may express the real relationship between the hippie's rejection of time and his rejection of possessions in Nick's terms: money entailed the constriction of experience, because when you had money you started to plan. Being without money and consequently living from minute to minute seemed, by contrast, an enrichment of personal experience: 'It makes you sort of respond more to your own sort of ideas.' Money conflicted with the idea of a natural and spontaneous existence.

It is easy to dismiss such attitudes as rationalisations. It may be true that hippies rejected money and possessions partly because they did not have them and were unwilling to do whatever would have to be done to acquire them, but the matter was not so simple. The sudden inheritance of wealth would shake even Nick's rejection of money and bring many other motivations into play, and it was this very possibility he feared. Hippies in any case fell into two categories. On the one hand there were those who could earn and save money, but who chose not to do so. For such people these attitudes and values were not really rationalisations. The others were those who could not earn and save money. Jimmy and Sue fell into this category. If they did get any money, then, like the heroes in the film *Easy Rider*, they 'blew it' in the search for immediate experience, whether as with Jimmy on three-day parties or as with Sue on methedrine. It is important to recall that Jimmy and Sue did admit that possessions held some attraction; they liked the idea of having 'nice things', but it paled before the possibilities of immediate experience.

There is another element. Many informants seemed ingenuously honest, but even among these there was a noticeable prevalence of what straight society would regard as crimes against property. Jimmy and Sue, for example, stole spontaneously and unthinkingly, but obviously enjoyed it. Gordon savoured the act. There was often some personal element in it, as when, for example, he left the stolen van unattended for a while one day only to have it recovered by the police and returned to its rightful owner. So that when he saw it in the street a few days later, he took the game one stage further and stole the van back. And Elaine relished the deceit when she entered pop festivals without paying.

This links to my previous argument because crime is itself a way of breaking down conventional categories and constraints. The hippies were breaking through the ossified rigidities of social form. They would claim that they were acting 'naturally', and just doing what everyone else would do if they dared. Their descriptions of their thefts or other crimes recalled Genet's remark that crime is the highest form of sensuality. Victims of theft or housebreaking, even though far away at the time of the act, often claim that they feel the theft as an invasion of themselves, almost a direct assault upon their person. Likewise, perhaps, the person responsible for the theft may feel it as an experience of heightened sensuousness: the thief is communicating vicariously with another person in a way that breaks through all nice values and civilised restraints.

Such an interpretation receives support from other forms of behaviour which might seem quite different. By coincidence, one thing that the two drug-dealers who figure in this book had in common was an attachment to craftsmanship and the handmade, particularly in furniture. Both sensed that property relationships are also, in a way, personal relationships, and they rejected the mass-produced because they could not *feel* anything of the maker or the previous owner. For Gordon this was part of the definition of the good society: 'a village or any area where you have one butcher, who feels that he is doing a service for everyone because there are always people around him who need meat. And you have one guy who puts shoes on horses, and that sort of thing, and you can identify with the person it's going to end up with.' We shall see in the next chapter how some pop groups sought this same possibility of personal identification in the relationship of audience and performer.

The capacity of goods to be a medium of communication between individuals, and often to assume sacramental significance in the process, finds obvious acknowledgment in the most varied religions and creeds, and the capacity of the thing to stand for the person may charge it with a sensuous and emotional content. Yet this possibility finds little acknowledgment in everyday life, as the hippies complained. So perhaps this represented, like theft and crime, an attempt to inject a heightened experience, both of intellectual meaning and emotional content, into everyday life.

Such an interpretation sees hippies as less novel and special than they are often taken to be. The personal component in exchanges of goods, the extent to which they stood for the giver and formed personal bonds and obligations between giver and receiver, was a characteristic of archaic society:

> A clan, household, association or guest are constrained to demand hospitality, to receive presents or to make blood and marriage alliances. The Dayaks have even developed a whole set of customs based on the obligation to partake of any meal at which one is present or which one has seen in preparation.
>
> The obligation to give is no less important. If we understood this we should also know how men came to exchange things with each other . . . To refuse to give, or to fail to invite, is—like refusing to accept—the equivalent of a declaration of war; it is a refusal of friendship and intercourse. Again, one gives because one is forced to do so, because the recipient has a sort of proprietary right over everything which belongs to the donor. The right is expressed and conceived as a sort of spiritual bond (Mauss, 1969, p. 11).

The ubiquitous passing of the marihuana cigarette around the hippie gathering, from one mouth to another, was felt to evoke just such a spiritual bond, slight and transitory though it might be. Similar expectations to those that Mauss described were working: the atmosphere of the occasion was usually such that for the host not to offer it to his guest or for his guest not to accept could be only interpreted as offensive. The same structure that appeared in tea-time at Carraghbay Terrace showed itself repeatedly in hippie gatherings, especially those where any sacramental object might be introduced such as food,

drugs or drink. Much of hippie behaviour can only be understood as an attempt to inject such a spiritual element into
material relationships.

THE EXPERIENCE OF OTHERS

In theory the hippie was supposed to espouse a generalised and
diffuse 'love', which was without particular or enduring object,
and which was more a matter of feeling than of action.
Sexual relations were supposed to be free and indulged without
commitment and without guilt, for immediate pleasure and
communication. Since love and sex were, when engaged in this
way, absolute goods, their direction and mode of expression were
never called into question. One consequence was that homosexuality and bisexuality could be accepted as readily as hetero-
sexuality. Another was the repudiation of the dominant
morality's exclusive identification of sexuality with genitality in
favour of a wider conception which approached the Freudian
notion of polymorphous perversity that the unsocialised child
was supposed freely to indulge.

It may have been true that among hippies the number and
variety of the individual's sexual relationships were greater
than among their 'straight' contemporaries, although I know of
nothing to indicate that the differences were substantial. A
large measure of any apparent difference may have been the
consequence of different degrees of 'visibility' of sexual activity.
What was important was that among hippies sex was approached
more casually and openly. On the one hand it reflected the
persistent accusation of hippie youth and their sympathisers that
the dominant society was hypocritical. On the other hand it
derived from and reflected the fact that the basic attitudes and
values of hippies forced them into a sort of innocence. Their
concern to break through empty forms and relationships, to
experience an undivided and total reality entailed an openness
and directness in this as in other things. Whether or not its
result was to trivialise the relationships involved remains a very
subjective judgment.

Between hip and straight, however, there remained more
similarity than difference in the underlying pattern of motivation.
The girls may have seemed more promiscuous than the majority

of their contemporaries, but, however much they enjoyed free and casual sex, in the end their deepest desire was to establish enduring relationships and to have children. The men admittedly did not share this willingness to settle, yet while Lucy's and Maggie's children were left fatherless, Gordon went through a transformation of his own as the arrival of his child approached: he gave up dealing, earned a small fortune driving a minicab all hours of the day and prepared to fill all a father's duties.

Where then does the difference lie? What is distinctive about the hippie's vision of personal and social relationships? To answer this, I shall focus on the unit which has come to embody all their aims and values in personal relationships—the commune.

The commune was the guiding image of a large part of hippie life, the nearest vision of the good society that was reached. In part it was pure ideology, a belief echoed through history that small numbers of people could discover freedom in a pastoral setting outside the constraints and frustrations of the social order: a negative freedom from the pressures of social time and routine and a positive freedom to lead a spontaneous and natural existence. In part it was also a matter of practical experience, an acknowledgment of the fact that the attempt to lead a different way of life within a tightly organised urban society imposed such pressures and conflicts that the attempt was doomed to rapid failure. Which factor was dominant varied from one situation to another: in England with its traditional tolerance of deviants and rebels, the former seemed uppermost, whereas the rural communes in the west of the United States developed relatively late in the hippie movement and seem to have been largely a response to the opposition that hippies felt in the cities.

The point at which a collection of people becomes a commune cannot be easily specified as a comparison of Maggie and Nick shows. On the one hand, the flat occupied by Lucy and Maggie was a commune, in that it was characterised by a relative informality of relationships and by the sharing of some property. Like most of the situations in which hippies lived, it had an essentially *accidental* character. People stayed there when it was convenient to do so, moving in and out without plan or purpose. As the group was characterised by a lack of deliberate form and structure over time, so also through space. A commune was in this sense the fortuitous consequence of the removal of the bench marks and boundaries the conventional man employs to divide up and impose meaning on his psychic and physical universe, in the measurement and planning of time or in the allocation of things to individual ownership. By contrast, the commune that Nick was trying to create was anything but accidental. It would be the Ideal City, built to utopian design. That it was designed to be free, loose and, in principle, open, should not obscure the fact that it was designed none the less.

There was here essentially the same division as appeared in planning time and acquiring possessions. There were those who found themselves incapable of planning and possessing, and for them some form of communal life was inevitable because they could not pursue any more organised and structured existence. Jimmy and Sue, and even Maggie and Gordon, had been insufficiently moulded by the processes of socialisation, and had become so absorbed in immediate experience that the acquisition of property and the deferral of gratification held no sway over them.

For many others, however, the origin was a rooted moral revulsion against what they called the 'heavy games' of life, the empty, formal and often ossified relationships of work, marriage, the street, indeed of that whole 'system' of which the dominant society supposedly consisted. This hippie element must be viewed with more scepticism, not over the honesty of the opinions but because of the position from which they were formed. Hippies became, by default or by design, *outsiders*. To the outsider, society is bound to appear a 'system', no more than a network of largely formal and empty relationships. Only the insider experiences their positive content, such comfort, warmth and communion as there is. What was important, however, was the belief that relationships within the dominant society were in this way empty and ossified, for the vision of the commune was above all the vision of conditions under which such a result might be avoided. The communal ideal was so constructed that it was the obverse of the image which the outsider held of the dominant society: an egalitarian sharing of goods and rights replaced the relationships of property and status; a total rejection of leadership and the attempt at collective decision-making replaced the dominant society's preoccupation with authority and hierarchy; above all the static role-relationships of work, marriage and family were replaced by a collective shouldering of the work and familial responsibilities of the commune members and by the autonomous freedom of each member outside this to 'do his own thing'.

To understand the true source and meaning of this vision of personal relationships, the time and circumstances under which Nick espoused the idea of a commune should be recalled. The commune was not chosen for its intrinsic virtues. It was chosen as the best means of cementing and preserving certain important personal relationships which a normal life in straight society could not sustain. The people with whom Nick wished to establish his commune were the people who had shared his transformation. He felt that he had been able to communicate with them in a depth and intimacy with which it would be impossible to communicate with others in the structured relationships of the dominant society: 'You experience reality with people you know really well—people with whom you've gone through the same experience.' For Nick, and for many like him, the commitment to communalism represented an attempt to develop a social environment within which the special kinds of personal relationships first experienced at the time of transformation might be developed and sustained. Necessarily such an environment would be as little as possible like the dominant society that was rejected and as conducive as possible to the kind of spontaneous experience that transformation involved. The commune's isolation, intimacy and sharing, and in particular its lack (in theory) of set form and structure made it obviously suitable. In principle at least, the commune should have allowed a specially direct mode of human communication, soul speaking to soul without the mediation of roles and institutions and similar social clutter.

Underlying this was a widespread belief that man discovers his true self in the moment of crisis and conflict, that he is what he shows himself to be in extreme situations. If it is correct that one is only truly oneself in such situations, it will follow that people can only fully communicate in the sharing of such extreme experiences.

It is in this way that the special depth and intensity of human relationship that the hippie claimed was realisable was intimately bound up with the possibility of that heightened mode of individual experience which we have seen encountered in the experience of transformation and which, as we shall see, was periodically retrieved through music, drugs or festivals.

THE PROBLEM OF ACTION

My argument so far in this chapter must have made the hippie seem a strangely passive creature. Time was neither saved nor spent; it was periodically abolished by transcendent experiences over which the individual had little control. Property and possessions were not just, or even mainly, things to be put to use, but rather symbols of shared meaning, obligation and communion. There was even a marked element of passivity in the hippie's conception of what constituted valuable human relationships. Such relationships were the product above all of those extreme situations when individuals found it possible to communicate in an absolute and immediate way. Here again there was something that was unsusceptible to human control, so that deliberate human action played little part.

All this seems strange to most people since no trait has been more characteristic of Western man than his commitment to action, his determination to load himself with work and to find in that the chief value of life. The hippie has sensed, however, that there might be something compulsive, even pathological, about such behaviour, so that in his own inactivity he could see a certain virtue. At any rate he was content that his psychic universe was dominated by sensations, ideas and images—of which he was largely the passive receptacle—rather than by purposes, intentions and actions. His concern was neither to explain the world nor to change it, but, above all, to experience it. Virtue was found in the capacity to be a good receptacle, not 'to do' but 'to be'; and to 'stay cool'—in one of its meanings to be able to go through a wide range of extreme experiences without being provoked into paranoid or frantic reactions or wanting to escape into compulsive activity.

At its broadest this may have derived from the belief of youth that they could find a wider domain of autonomy and freedom in the realms of passive experience than in those of deliberate action. Such a belief would have been dramatically novel. Traditionally Western man has seen the realm of sensation and experience as relatively given and uncontrollable, whereas the field of human action has been construed as the real domain of freedom. Have these roles now been reversed? May it just be that in an advanced industrial society the young have come to find their margins of freedom in sense and experience just because social action has become an area of compulsion and constraint? Such a possibility should at least be entertained.

Yet experience alone was not enough. However much hippies might focus on sensual receptivity, most of them sometimes felt a need for purposeful activity. For conventional man this of course posed no problem: by accepting the contemporary patterns of work and leisure, and the routine behaviours of collective life, he had available a framework for meaningful social action. When, as for hippies, this was not available, action itself became a problem. Another framework had to be found. They all understood the problem, and felt themselves in danger of 'letting the whole thing run', and ending up just lying in a room on a mattress all day. How was this incapacity avoided, and a pattern developed which would substitute for conventional work and leisure?

For the clue to the solution it is necessary to dwell a little on behaviour in the period immediately after transformation. What happened to Nick, John and Jeremy, the three whose experience has been considered? Each became totally absorbed in some essentially private and individual mission. Jeremy led a student revolt on his university campus. John suddenly flew from Singapore to London, to spend every penny of his money and moment of his time in the promotion of Instant Karma. Nick got so completely 'into his own thing', in pursuing a personal interpretation of art that his teachers gave him up. Each embarked upon a mission, a personally motivated and somehow deeply absorbing activity. What is more, each worked desperately hard at it, and gave to it total commitment of a special sort.

It is easy to say that during this period each of them was seriously unbalanced. That is probably correct if one understands by 'balance' the moderately pleasant and wholly bearable life of the straight person, which is so divided in time and in space between the different spheres of family, work and leisure, that it is never quite proper, nor indeed possible, to be totally involved in any one. Commitment there may be. That is quite proper. But that open enthusiasm and full absorption of the kind that Nick, Jeremy and John discovered, is another matter. It is kept at a safe distance, reserved, if at all, for certain social roles of a special kind, like the artist or the professional footballer. Since of necessity it undermines the possibility of objective and rational judgment, it is believed in the normal person to be somehow deeply seditious.

Jeremy, John and Nick admitted, in retrospect, that during this period each of them was unbalanced, and in a sense slightly mad. John, for example, realised he had thrown away a lot of money in a totally futile exercise; Nick came to realise that what had absorbed him was only a small part of what might be involved in the creation of works of art, and Jeremy realised that the rebellion he was leading had lost all relationship to its supposed causes. In material terms each of them lost a good deal.

But none of them regretted the experience. Jeremy enjoyed the time 'immensely more' than his last year at school, and Nick felt that he learned a lot more from doing it his way. John, when met again months later, now with a straight job as a clerk and much less the hippie, felt that things were better in that it was good to have a measure of stability, security and sensible proportion in his life. But should the opportunity occur again he would not have a moment's hesitation in throwing all this away in favour of that old absorption and commitment. He had no doubt of the reason: 'Then at least I felt alive.'

It is just as important to understand how such periods of extremity could come about as to recognise that they could be enjoyed. The possibility of their kind of autonomous and creative commitment was dependent upon the prior breakdown and disintegration of the reality structure by which they had previously been working. That structure represented the cumulative consequence of the numberless dimensions of socialisation. Against this the new mode of activity stood in striking contrast. Nick was right to perceive it as egocentric. The importance of the first stage of transformation—the disintegration of the previous structure of social reality—was that it engendered in those who experienced it the *enthusiasm to do something themselves*. They became capable, in a literal sense, of 'doing their own thing, in their own time'.

It will be well to dwell a moment on the implications of this expression. It certainly implied freedom, but of a special kind: not just negative freedom, *from* restraint, but a positive freedom *to* discover one's own fulfilment. There was the implication also that 'doing their own thing' would for the majority of people be different from the things they now did: in other words that the possibility of fulfilment was represented by some inner truth, something obscured by the hustle of everyday activity. It also implied an absorption and commitment, of a kind to which the individual was prepared to see his whole identity linked. Another expression adds further clarification. They often spoke of 'getting into' something and there was a literal emphasis on the 'into'. 'Getting into mysticism' or 'Getting into music' implied not just joining a particular group of people in some activity. It carried also the suggestion that one's self would become fully absorbed in it, at both a physical and intellectual level. It was apparent when the hippie spoke of someone 'not really being into something', that he meant that this full commitment of the self had not been made, that the involvement was not of thought *and* feeling together.

What I am suggesting is that the hippie managed to some extent to evolve a mode of activity which was characteristic of what might be called, to adapt Eliot's term, an undissociated sensibility. It was first discovered in the missionary activity following transformation. It was intense, spontaneous and often irrational, acknowledging no constraints outside the individual actor and his own commitment. This experience was the model for the style of activity that the hippie subsequently espoused. In the older hippie whose transformation was long passed, the new mode of activity came close to some traditional conceptions of unalienated labour. This was clearly expressed by Neil, an informant who spent much of his time that summer helping to organise a pop festival from his flat a few streets from Carraghbay Terrace:

I mean everybody's happy to work, and I worked my arse

off, I mean some days when we were putting that festival together I was working fourteen hours a day, and nothing would induce me to work fourteen hours a day if I didn't want to. I was thoroughly enjoying myself. On one level I was really sort of twitchy and worried, and like very upset on another because it was incredibly hard and tiring work. It's not work that anyone's hung up about it's who you work for. I mean there are some people who don't want to work, but they're going to have to eventually—if you go to any freak's pad if they lay there long enough and the garbage piles higher and higher until one day they have to take all the garbage out, and it becomes an amazing hive of industry. *It's not a fact of totally not working, it's a question of doing it when you feel like it, how you feel like it and to what extent you feel like it.*

There is, however, a subtle twist of emphasis from the usual positions. The proprietary relationship in the product of labour, and even the employment relationship itself, have slipped from the centre of the stage. For Neil and other hippies, unlike previous generations of social critics, attention is now explicitly focused on the quality of immediate experience.

However this mode of work is defined, what is important is its origin. None of the people whose lives I have considered seemed before their transformation to be characterised by this particularly autonomous and spontaneous mode of activity. Transformation had broken down the conventional pattern of socially-structured action, and engendered the enthusiasm to do something themselves. Of the immediate results of transformation, one was permanent and the other transitory. What was permanent was that acquired capacity to engage in a pattern of activity which was autonomous and spontaneous, and which could have for the actor meaning and structure other than that which was socially determined. What was certainly more transitory and more vulnerable was the enthusiasm required to sustain it, and this perhaps may be the core of a doubt, which we must in due course pursue.

CONCLUSION

The broad areas of behaviour examined in this chapter were

chosen only because together they seemed to yield a reasonably full picture of the hippie's life, and the beliefs and values which motivated it. I have suggested a fundamental consistency of characteristics from one area of life to another, and a basic similarity in the configurations into which they fall: avoidance of stable and formal relationships and behaviour; rejection of whatever was deliberate or purposeful or had any goal outside itself; and above all, preoccupation with those modes of intensified experience where intellectual and sensuous awareness were most intimately joined.

For the particular pattern described I suggested two possible sources. One was that traditional bedrock of bohemian perceptions and values outlined in the Introduction. Another, more important, was the process of transformation, and the particular modes of experience and behaviour it opened up. They probably cannot, even together, account for the full configurations of attitude and behaviour, but they do define certain fundamental modes of perception and feeling which in time infiltrated most areas of the individual's life, as he tried to consolidate them into some reasonably coherent and consistent meaning. This process of consolidation was for the most part not deliberate or intentional. The individual was seldom conscious of the channels into which he was drawn, still less of the way he was drawn there by previous experience and the imprint it left of loves and desires and fears.

V

THE SACRAMENTS OF RENEWAL

Any community, however small, requires social services and welfare agencies of some kind. However diffuse and decentralised, it will also depend on a certain number of organisers and entrepreneurs. Equally any culture, even one emphasising diversity and spontaneity, requires a group of people who will define and interpret its values and goals, and minister the fundamental sacraments which sustain it. In some cases these two roles are united, perhaps most often in small or archaic societies. In industrial societies, by contrast, they more usually display a high degree of differentiation and specialisation. Between economic and welfare roles on the one hand, and those of ritual and sacrament on the other, there is explicit separation.

Among hippies there was generally little separation. There were certain roles among them that were important and around these tended to cluster both economic and ritual functions. The two most important were the provision of drugs and underground music.

These roles are explored in this chapter. The account of them necessarily covers a large part of the culture and social arrangements of these people. I shall try to show the way sacramental and economic roles were linked together and gave expression to the perceptions, experiences and values already described.

It is not possible to say with certainty why these economic and sacramental roles were linked. One relationship, however, was clear: the sacramental role of drugs and underground music—and the special esteem assigned to those who provided them—derived from their role in transformation, and from the fact that, among the sources of transcendental experience, they were particularly accessible and effective. The fact that industrial technology made them capable of easy reproduction or communication meant that they were readily available for the re-enactment or renewal of transformation. From this derived their sacramental role and the particular character of much of hippie ritual.

Drugs and music may have been the focus of ritual, but they were also the basis of material livelihood. This was because they were the two commodities, easily produced or acquired by hippies, which found a ready market in the wider society outside. Estimates of the number of people in the United Kingdom who have used cannabis, for example, have ranged as high as one million. Not all of these supplies have passed through the hands of hippies or the underground, but at one point or another enough has done so to provide them with a sufficient economic basis. The groups who provided heavy rock and some other varieties of music were also often sufficiently close to hippie and underground communities for the communities to profit from the sales of the groups' records: a group was not just those people who appeared on stage, it required others to drive vans, handle amplification, design record covers, even arrange performances or negotiate contracts. It was from such activities that a good proportion of hippies gained a livelihood.

The leaders and entrepreneurs, the drug-dealers, the pop groups and the early festival organisers are important because their beliefs and behaviour most fully illuminate the underlying structure and goals of hippie society. They are important, also, because they were the people who were most often in contact with the institutions of the dominant society, and they had consequently to spend much of their time negotiating between the different realities of hip and straight.

MUSIC

So what we're into is letting people know that they can get it together. We just like to create a feeling, like if you've seen the band then perhaps you get the feeling that the band has that feeling, and I have that feeling, when the band is playing music. It's just like a happy feeling, you know you can be happy, you know you can smile. Maybe everything is crumbling down around you, and all those other bum trips are happening, all those other bum financial things, but you're listening to something good, and you can turn onto it free.

Pop music is an essential element of the 'underground' and a central preoccupation of most adolescent hippie groups. It is of course much more: the core element in what is sometimes described as youth culture, it holds an appeal to groups far outside it in age and life-style. It is then somewhat surprising that such music should be the main medium of cultural expression of the very special groups with whom this study is concerned. It is even more surprising because pop music is now established and commercial, and deeply entwined in the dominant order of our society. But the concern here is only with a certain type of pop music, played in a special context for rather particular purposes. What distinguished the musicians among my informants from the generality of pop groups will quickly become apparent.

Everyone, remarked Elaine, had a guitar, but who played? Her observation was accurate, but she missed the point. The guitar was not, as in the straight world, an instrument for the exercise of defined professional skills. It was at once a vehicle and a symbol. How and why was this so? What was the central meaning of their music to those involved in it, and particularly to those to whom they communicated it? How did they become musicians, and why did they continue? How did music act to amplify, reinforce and sustain the experience of transformation? How did it function to draw outsiders together and hold them together, and often forge of them a markedly special cultural phenomenon? How far did it provide a vehicle to promote that configuration of values examined in the previous chapter?

In exploring these questions our guides now are Phil and Jerry and Doug. Phil was the heart of a group called The Purple Phantoms, and Jerry its head. Doug was the leader of Federalearth Freaks. Among the thirty people interviewed at length, seven were involved all their time in pop music. We follow Phil, Jerry and Doug because they were the three most certainly involved, the others being concerned in more supporting roles. We follow them also because they lived in the Ladbroke Grove area of London, close to most of the other people in this book, who identified with their music.

The mission

There are thousands of pop groups in Britain, most of which have transitory and anonymous lives: with the possible exception of the cinema, it is after all the chief contemporary medium of artistic expression. Equally important, if you are very good or very lucky, it is not impossible to make a lot of money. Federalearth Freaks and the Purple Phantoms were on this score a little special as were most groups with some implicit or explicit 'underground' link: their relationship to the dominant society and particularly to the commercial world was intrinsically more ambiguous, and if money and wordly success were strong motives for entering the music world, they were subsequently rationalised or sublimated into commitments of a quite different nature. Around their music-making role developed not simply a predictable sense of personal attachment and identity but also a missionary purpose that could acquire almost magical significance. It was this that allowed them to act as unifiers of the hippie world and reinforcers of its culture.

One must begin where they began, with entry into the music world. Phil of the Purple Phantoms was typical. Aged twenty-two, rotund and cherubic, a look of innocent ferocity, he explained:

> The only thing I believe in is my guitar. I was a student until I was 18 and finished school, and then I did 30 different jobs in a year to get some money together, to get some equipment and new instruments and stuff. Then when I was about 19 that was it. And I just kept playing.

For anyone, whatever his social situation, a sense of identity may come through the feelings of personal growth accompanying development as a musician. What is more remarkable is that the initiation into music-making came to be endowed with a quasi-mystical aura. Doug of the Federalearth Freaks described how he began to play the guitar:

> I'd been playing instruments since I was about six years old. Piano, violin, trombone and drums and all that type of thing, but I'd never really found an instrument that

clicked, but then one day, I was on a Spanish island, it
came as a revelation—gotta play the guitar—it was as easy
as that. So what am I doing here, wasting my time? So
I went back to New Zealand and I joined the Conserva-
torium. Then I had a different teacher, then I went to
America and studied jazz improvisation with other
teachers—and classical teachers—and after I had learnt it
all I went to another island in Greece, and spent two
years just by myself on this island surrounded by pistachio
trees and peacocks, just putting it all together, and then
I came to London and got the band together.

The sense of transformation is here specifically formulated.
Implicit, although hardly less clear, are all the phases of self-
preparation for spiritual mission: along with revelation comes
absolute commitment, to be followed by arduous self-training
and spiritual growth pursued alone and in silence. Phil's
belief in the spiritual role and significance of his musical
instrument and the music he played was not rare. Doug's
almost messianic formulation of it probably was. But the
distance from the one to the other was not great: for both
Phil and Doug the beginnings of their music-making were
shrouded with something approaching a sense of illumination
and rebirth.

Such commitment might come suddenly, but for Doug and
probably for many others it was the termination—temporary
at least—of a long period of alienation. It was the final port of
call at the end of a Childe Harolde's Pilgrimage, the end of a
desperate search for the self:

When I left school I went into advertising. Then I'd go
right round the world hitch-hiking, and I'd come back to
New Zealand and I'd take a job. I'd do that for six months
and I'd think 'This is just so nauseating', and at the end of
six months I'd say 'I've got to leave again', so I leave
New Zealand and I hop on a freight boat or banana boat,
or something, and go somewhere else, and travel around.

I went to New York, I worked there, I sold tickets at
one of those strip places on Times Square, it was really
repulsive. Also selling really commercial paintings in

Greenwich Village. People would do these terrible paintings and the guy would give him £5 for the painting and
he would sell it for £150, and I had to sell the paintings
and tell people who didn't know anything about painting,
I had to talk them into it, that it was great and they
should have it in their bathrooms and sure enough they'd
pay £150 and I'd get commission. It was dreadful.

So you'd leave it and the next thing you'd hitch-hike
round and there were a lot of places I hardly needed any
money at all, I mean I lived very cheaply, just finding out
about life, as Gorky says 'The University of Life', just
going around and finding what's what, and what was one
looking for in life. I mean I was enjoying my life, but I
was thinking what in the hell am I on this planet for—
what's happening—you can be happy, but you can still not
know what you're doing, and after all being happy is not
quite enough, it's like you want something a bit more
rewarding.

A subsequent sense of transformation and mission would be
a fitting conclusion to such an odyssey. The account itself was
no doubt accurate and truthful but how far also was the sense
of illumination, commitment and calling? It is possible that
such accounts were stock myths for the consumption of their
public, to be confirmed even in private conversation. That
would put their audiences in the role of children who would
follow Pied Piper if he only struck the right millennial note. In
the context of what they subsequently said, that did not seem
quite right. The more likely answer is that in these accounts
they were being truthful but not accurate. That they did not
really experience it in quite that way is almost certain, but that
they should now believe it is entirely consistent. If they did
believe it, one must deduce either that their outsider status,
relatively homeless situation and uncertain grasp of everyday
reality had markedly deluded them; or that there was something special about the music they played and their private
relationship to it and to their audiences that led them to conceive its origins in such a special way. Each factor was an
element of the explanation. For the former the argument of
preceding chapters provides some support. To understand the

latter it is necessary to turn to the accounts of what happened when they began to play.

Making magic

Popular music has often been the vehicle for a collective lowering of inhibitions. When my informants were in their cradles Johnny Ray was evoking in their mothers a maternal hysteria they might well have envied. In their childhood Elvis Presley was beginning that blatant exploitation of sex in which most pop singers since have followed him, with substantially the same result: an orgy of stomping, shouting and screaming, a cathartic release of aggression. The remoteness of the performer and the undeveloping nature of the interaction between him and the audience, however, generally made the whole ritual safe and aseptic. With increasing commercialisation, conventional pop became almost clinical.

This was the inevitable backdrop to the activity of underground groups. In a sense they were only carrying a general movement for the structured lowering of inhibitions to a particular extreme. But extremity is the point: at a certain stage the change in degree becomes a change also in form and content. The release of inhibitions may become mildly addictive: tolerance builds up, and there is a need to go further and further for the same sensation. One could argue that the Purple Phantoms, Federalearth Freaks and their underground fellows were just the hardline addicts of pop, with the bourgeois sense of proportion and balance removed. That may be true, although the evidence of their behaviour does not fully support it. In any event it is too limited an explanation and is largely to miss the point: what is important for understanding their activity is what they were trying to do and why, and what they believed about themselves.

> *Phil:* What we're doing, like our current Purple Phantom trip, is turning people on. The only way we know how to turn them on is just to play.
> *Jerry:* Creating the awareness, but not in the sort of average sense of going out and saying to people 'Hey, there's this awareness'; kids don't pick up on that. All the

band is doing is playing good music and giving out good vibes, and turning people on; you got people standing around in a hall, not even saying hey it sounds good, but standing there smiling and bopping about and like not questioning the guitarist's ability and all those other fucking things; we want to take people right away from that, you know, have them grooving on just listening to the music. They learn to derive good times from just listening to basic music and not getting hung up with all the other trips, because those other trips are not being thrown at them. Nobody's got hung up about the fact that the place is a hole or any of those other fucking things. And they do acknowledge this awareness. We've seen it happen, because the band has just stepped into situations, we've done some free gigs, unannounced, and with the first number everybody's up, standing on their feet, clapping, jumping about, smiling, yelling for more.

What we've done is put that element of surprise in their lives, which maybe they all need. It's like a little present, man, somebody gives you a little present. And it turns you on. And maybe they'll begin to surprise people in their turn.

And not only that. They change. Something which turned them on the night before doesn't any more. They go and see another band and the situation on the stage, giving out the vibes, suddenly doesn't turn them on any more. They've had something happening that isn't blasting hype at them and isn't sort of laying heavy trips on them. Because they really don't want to know about them.

There's a spiritual wave creeping over people, people want to get back to the earth, man, you know they really want to know what it's like to be alive. It's really a quasi-political situation which exists with certain bands. See, we found that by doing this for people, we have kids coming up to us, and us coming on to kids, just openly. You very rarely get people moving down the street here smiling: you say hello to certain people and they seem offended. It's very sort of closed . . . it's a land of the fucking bed-sitter, and we'd really like to help them get out of their bed-sitter.

Jerry was an agent of transformation. He and his group knew what they were doing, or at least what they were trying to do. There were elements common to all the experiences examined in previous chapters: the ubiquitous notion of 'turning on', the sudden intuition, the transcending of rational standards and structured judgment—there was mystical illumination or there was nothing, and the explicit linking of mental and physical dimensions—to be 'smiling and bopping about and not questioning, to know what it is to be alive'. Jerry's particular way of describing what he was doing tells us something more. He was, paradoxically, forcing people to relax, something that could only be done by catching them by surprise. Jerry was right to see the importance of the element of surprise. It was the way in which, above all others, the individual was most easily transported from the 'heavy trip' realm of intentional and rational behaviour and purposeful activity. The realm they entered was transcendental and mystical: they were, in Mrs Adams' words, taken 'out of themselves'. This realm has always been a common and integral part of everyday life. What was surprising was that for them the everyday world appeared so 'heavy' and behaviour within it so exacting, that to be transported beyond it seemed something magical.

Doug was different, not because the magic he was concerned to evoke was in its nature significantly different, but because he was more concerned to categorise and articulate what he believed to be happening. To speak of being 'intoxicated' and 'high' is clinical and contemporary. With 'consciousness', 'ecstasy', the 'blissful' and the 'divine', one sees the phenomenon hesitantly set within a traditional mystical framework.

It's a thing with electricity and it's a thing also with the audience and how they're reacting, and what the vibrations and maybe what the astrological signs are, or who knows? But some nights are very, very special and the audience are like tinder and you're igniting it and it explodes and the audience becomes the musicians and the musicians become the audience and everybody's ecstatic and very blissful, and this may happen maybe once out of every ten concerts or something like that, but they're so different from the average concert . . . I mean then most people enjoy it and they clap, and they've enjoyed themselves, but it's nothing. They don't know what it can really be like. And we haven't got that much control over it, it's something that just happens when the time's ripe. I mean I always try to sing, I put everything into it, every performance as much as I can but sometimes it just really takes off and then—it's like everybody in the audience—it's like they're intoxicated completely, I mean they are really high from the music and from the vibrations, and getting them to sing with us and clap with us, and so if everybody joins in we build up this fantastic feeling, and it's just real crazy, because everybody's been bubbling. But what goes into it, it's just impossible to say. You can't say what the ingredients are. It's a strange power.

So all of a sudden there comes a point like last night, the last number did it. We played for an hour and we usually take an hour and a half and the last five minutes it was just like that. You just did it, you just feel it.

It's not always like that. You really have to win the audience over and to make out and let them break through their inhibitions so that they're enjoying themselves without intellectualising, because most people who go to hear music are sitting and listening and thinking this is this, and that's that, and it's sort of like . . . But you can't do that with music, you've got to not think about it, you've got to relax into it.

Because we try, you know, we try from the beginning that hard, but they don't realise we're trying that hard. They take it for granted. They just think you're just jumping around the stage or something, but emotionally you've really given out tremendously. Where a good audience—in those blissful moments, they recharge you when you're on stage, you get this fantastic thing coming from the audience, it's like you're not doing anything at all—it's so easy, because you're riding on the crest of their power and you can imagine two or three thousand people have got a lot of electricity going out there if they can conduct it, channel it, that's what it is because it's usually very dispersed, everybody's head's somewhere else, they're not together, no one's together, consciousness is just sprayed around, but that's what we try to do, bring it to one thing and channel it.

And when we do, it's like a wave of faces, you sort of suddenly see teeth everywhere instead of lips, and you suddenly see people's hands are moving and their bodies are just, I mean it's amazing, like the expression on their faces, you know, it's very rewarding, seeing them sort of sitting up there. First, they've got their arms folded for the first ten minutes, then next after half an hour maybe a few of them are flicking their fingers and tapping their feet and then the last thing they break through and, you know, they really let go. And that's how they should be after the first five minutes and we played it to that intensity in the first five minutes. We have broken our inhibitions, we're completely free, but we've got to bring them on our trip, we've got to transcend the audience.

The function of such an event is not merely to 'entertain', to use the term that most fully expresses what the contemporary mind understands by leisure. Nor is it simply to provide a safety-valve for the release of inhibitions in the way that much popular music always has. In enabling performers and audience alike to break out of their specific roles, and be joined in a common activity felt to forge mystical bonds, it comes nearer to an act of communal worship. This is not such an inappropriate comparison as at first appears, for at least some theorists of leisure, such as Joseph Pieper (1952), have always argued that divine worship is a fuller and more complete experience of leisure than conventional entertainment and recreation.

Such a performance has several special characteristics. Whereas until recently a performer would establish and depend upon a clear line between himself and the audience, there was here a deliberate attempt to blur the line and reduce distance and separation. The performer moved from his segmented, specific role to become a living being whom the audience wanted to know personally and who wanted to be known personally.

There was a change also in the nature of the audience. Instead of being critical or appreciative or questioning, it was participatory. It had become committed to the performer as a symbolic figure. The performer took the audience on his trip. He was a leader who renewed and reinforced the fundamental goals and aspirations of his audience. The performers' power resided in the very fact that they had broken through their inhibitions, slewed off their particular social identity with its purposive and rational restraint and self-control. They had become free, and for their freedom and spontaneity, and particularly for its shameless and explicit exposure, they became the archetypal heroes of transformation. When Doug spoke of transcending the audience, what he meant was that the group had to break them down and reinforce their previous experiences of transformation. The audience, like the performers, came to a concert alienated and lost, the magic of original transformation increasingly the subject of attrition by everyday life. It was this process that the performers halted and swung into reverse. In the process they became the renewers of transformation and occasionally its initiators.

Members of the audience were thus transformed anew, and for this they repaid its agent with love and awe. At such an event, wrote Bennett Berger (1971), an audience could 'offer waves of love to a performer in exchange for his affirmation of them'. Doug described it in a similar way: in those blissful moments the audience recharged you and you rode on the crest of their power.

The social foundation of change

Outside of time and the dominant social order, some pop groups then pursued their role of moral entrepreneur, agents of a new utopia. How did this missionary activity relate to other dimensions of their lives? Jerry has given an optimistic assessment, probably more so than the facts warranted. He was drawing people into a new sort of community, out of their bed-sitter world. The kids came up to him in the street and said 'Hello', and when he said 'Hello' to them they were not offended and evasive. It had not been easy. London was behind the great centres of pop in America, but the change was coming.

The last three years in England, I can say I've met less

people, and known far less people, than say my first week of wandering around Frisco, or my first few days of being in New York. Because I've had the opportunity to open myself up to less people. Because I've had to contend with those small little scenes.

The society from which Federalearth Freaks and the Purple Phantoms had dropped out was a world dominated by the nuclear family of husband, wife and children. It was a family-centred and even child-centred society. The family pursued its life in relative secrecy and isolation, and, with increasing geographical and social mobility, its ties to the broader community were perhaps weaker than in the past. Rejection of the nuclear family was pervasive among outsider groups. Alienation from the dominant society often mirrored or was mediated by estrangement from their own family. They often came from unhappy family backgrounds, where the absence of links between the family and the wider society meant that there was little opportunity for relief or support for the hapless young victim trapped by family tensions. Among outsider groups a whole ideology emerged around the rejection of the nuclear family. Even for those who had not come from such troubled backgrounds, the nuclear family was the symbol of everything bourgeois—flat, toneless, sterile and utterly normal. Neither Doug nor Phil nor Jerry came in fact from a disturbed family background, but, being immersed in hippie roles and values, were almost inevitably caught up in the common aspiration to give new meaning to the concepts of family and community.

The way they did this is deeply revealing of their moral and economic role, because it was modulated most forcibly by their subjective experience of life within their own music group and within the underground to which it was attached. The 'family' was for them that group, relatively large in number but concentrated in geographical area, with whom they were in constant communication and who were related in some way to their music. They were: 'People who I consider my brothers and sisters, the people who are involved in this, they're sort of like brothers and sisters and most of them live around the neighbourhood.' Doug's family—his 'brothers and sisters'— were all those people who played some part in this shared

activity of producing music. They included those who drove
the vans, handled amplification and technical matters, designed
record covers, and many others. Money came from the commercial world directly to the group, but thereafter they 'spread
it around' in payment for services of one kind or another. It
was almost like the position at periods in the past when household servants were included in the definition of members of
the family.

The things that were done together and the quality of
personal relationships within the group were important in the
ways that close relationships commonly are important.

> We get together at one of these places and sit round,
> we'll sing these Chants which have word combinations
> passed up through thousands of years and there's all the
> magical connotations that if you say a certain vibration of
> words together, over and over and over, that you build up
> this fantastic feeling of vibration, and that's really very
> enlightening and very stimulating. We might do that for
> six or seven hours non-stop and maybe we'll only do that
> on a Sunday—we'll do it, two or three of us at our home
> or they'll do it at their house, but we do get together and do
> this and this is a big part of our leisure. (Doug)

There was something more. Because of the group's special
sense of role and mission, personal relationships within the
group were considered particularly important in their relationship to the world outside it. The success of the band was seen
to be deeply related to the success of its 'family' as a community. Among all outsider groups, the sincerity and depth of
personal relationships is always in some sense, an 'issue'.
Where the outsiders were entrepreneurs who believed they were
helping to give, by quasi-mystical means, a new emotional tone
to individual and group experience, they assumed particular
importance. It was quite possible to take a detached and professional view of the matter: whether the harmony and well-
being of the family was the primary concern, or simply the
success of the band in communicating the right feelings to its
audiences, was immaterial. The two were interdependent, as
Jerry saw:

All we want to do, all our family wants, the family surrounding the band, we just want to have the band play the
band's music, and enjoy itself playing the band's music.
All those other trips, they'll either go down or come up.
All that has to happen is that the band and its immediate
family maintains a happy balance, because if you're main-
taining a happy balance and a happy situation, that's what
people pick up.

What went for the Purple Phantoms went equally for
Federalearth Freaks. Since as a band their concern was to
liberate people from the confines of their own 'ego-trips',
the relationships within the family were critically important. The
slight element of anxiety and tentativeness on this point by
Federalearth Freaks reflected this: everyone went through
difficult periods, said Doug, and some were more worldly than
others, but basically he believed they were getting closer all
the time, the members of the 'family' getting steadily more
'brotherly'.

Personal relationships within the 'family' were, then, important to the band's mission. It may have been that the audience
would pick up good or bad 'vibes' within the band, but this
was not all there was to it, and it was not the end of the inter-
relationship of family and mission. Three more specific aspects
recurred.

First, relationships within the band's family had to be
spontaneous and not calculative. If the relationships were
based on rational consideration of profit and loss, they became
empty and sterile, mirroring relationships within the dominant
social order. They could not go about their mission of turning
people on to a higher reality if they were enchained to that of
material advantage.

> We're not really conscious of the things members of the
> family do for us or we do for them. It's just like in terms
> of being together: us being around their pad, us meeting
> them in the street, us being together. I really dig to get out
> of a 'them and us' situation, I would just like it to be us all
> the time. You know, at Hyde Park, man, 500,000 people
> in the fucking park, and at no given moment probably
> in an immediate circle of 100 did any more than 2 or 3 of

them know any more than 2 or 3 of the others. What a shame. What a waste. Or even you know attempt to get past that sort of thing. It really is a waste.

And that's like another illusion that we're in the process of trying to run people onto: helping them find out, just tripping around, maybe just turning a hundred people on, a couple of hundred people on, working the same magic as you work. Like I wish a lot more people would turn me on to a lot more free things. It's really a gas. You really appreciate it. But there's that old wives' tripper you know don't give anybody anything 'cause like they really won't appreciate it, and they'll laugh at you behind your back.

The other factors were closely related, and they lead back quite explicitly to now familiar issues: the segmentation of roles, the concept of personality and the constraint of enthusiasm. Phil had begun the discussion of the 'family' with a categorical rejection of segmented roles: what marked the band out as different, what provided the key to their way of living, was that there was no distinction between the spheres of work, family and leisure, with their different attendant personalities: 'You know, there's no separation between the band and the family. What we do is what we live. There's no two separate identities of us on stage and us at home at all.'

With less precision Jerry would go on to detect in this, and more particularly in the closeness of the members of the 'family', the key to change. He perceived that the individual identity of each member of the family, when not divided among over-lapping roles and commitments, but totally channelled into the united commitment of the family, was what made enthusiasm possible and thus effected change. It was this involvement and enthusiasm which he objectified as a 'spiritual wave'.

You know, there's something about getting things done: a tight unit can just unify things, can get certain things done a lot faster than one or two individuals spreading around. It's a whole sort of spiritual wave that's coming, and that people are becoming more and more aware of, but it needs a unification—bodies of people to start things shaking again.

Within the family, then, things were, in a dimly perceived way, somehow different: their rejection of segmented roles and commitment to spontaneity and enthusiasm may have made them innocent agents of social change. At least it enabled them to provide rituals capable of sustaining and extending the values, goals and commitments of their constituents. Phil, Jerry and Doug would probably never achieve that fame and fortune in the heavy world of pop which underneath it all, perhaps, they really most of all desired. Their continuing commitment to outsiders and the underground probably reflected this. Clearly, however, there was consolation in being part of a spiritual wave—even if one that was unlikely ever to engulf the world.

The commercial world

Pop groups thus held a key position within the culture. They helped minister and uphold that experience of transformation which underlay it, provided the forms and rituals through which its goals and values found expression, and, in the process, established the minimal degree of social and economic organisation necessary to sustain them. All these factors gave them a position of leadership which partly strengthened, and partly itself flowed from, their final role, that of negotiating between the different realities of hip and straight.

This final role was in any case bound to be theirs, so long as pop music represented a major leisure industry of the dominant society, and the nature of the relationship between underground pop groups and the dominant social order, within which and against which they worked, was bound to be both critical and ambiguous.

The relationship was primarily with the commercial record companies. It was conducted at many levels. On the one hand, the record companies held the key to certain kinds of success, and almost every group, however much they might deny it, would have succumbed willingly to financial success. On the other hand the groups had an élitist sense that, important as money was to them, it was not everything. They were artists and missionaries of a sort, and had to keep it at a distance:

You meet a lot of people who are obviously just in it in a very worldly and gross sense, and being among those people I find a bit of a bring-down, so I try to spend as little time as possible with people who give out bad vibes. In this business, they're not exactly racketeers, but they're promoters, and it's obviously absolutely only a business, and you're like in a sausage machine and they're pumping you out. It's a question of discrimination and one has to be very discriminating, and it's up to oneself how much one involves oneself in it.

Maybe Doug was able to maintain such detachment because his earlier experience of selling and advertising had given him some understanding of how the heavy commercial world operated and he could chart a course through it which preserved the essential integrity of his role. Phil and Jerry, by contrast, were innocents abroad in a world of formal commitments and commercial arrangements. Five-year contracts were not the best context within which to surprise people. Phil's antipathy to the money-world found expression in fantasies which must surely have made his commercial promoter weep at his innocence.

I'd like to do something like get the Albert Hall or something and just completely surround every floor with drinks and food and sell tickets for a pound a time and when everybody comes through the door they get a little envelope with their pound back.

Phil was not allowed to do this. For the most part the groups had to toe the line, because the record companies were the arbiters of fame and fortune, and, as they knew, such fame and fortune was partly the source of their symbolic status and moral and economic role in their own culture. But they could not go too far: if they did, they would be thought to have copped out, and might find they had sacrificed their sure underground constituency for an uncertain future. In the end, however, calculations of this kind were not what determined the relationship between groups and record companies. Frameworks of purpose and commitment were fundamentally at variance, and it was this which made occasional conflict inevitable.

The Purple Phantoms were absorbed in the openness, spontaneity and hedonism of the hip creed. They could not plan ahead, and would have repudiated such a way of living even if they were capable of it. The groups were involved in the pursuit of a momentary, absolute transcendence, in breaking through and making others let go. For them there was only that moment. The record companies by contrast needed to know where they were. They could work only on the basis of secure and explicit long-term agreements, which were moreover part of the route to success for the performers themselves. But while the groups willed the end, they could not will the means.

The conflicts were generally trivial and petty, and often unpleasant. What is most instructive, however, is the process of rationalisation by which the underground groups chose to explain them, and the particular techniques by which they tried to resolve them.

Jerry: Well, in our last group we never made a penny, I mean we sold a lot of records but we never made a penny, because of that whole record company bullshit commercial game. We were the fools.

We got done. To put it mildly, we got done. But uh, bits of paper, man. Like that's another reason why we just dig to turn people on to music, why we want to play for free, 'cause there's a whole little world that just exists on fucking bits of paper. It's the little bits of paper that hang you up, all your life. They can really make life a misery for you. Sign your name! Where's that at? Where's that to sign your name on a piece of paper that will completely screw you up for the next four or five years. Where's that one at?

Phil: We were screwed up for a year and a half, or two years. As it is it's going to cost us a mild amount of bread to get out of this contract, so we can play for free, so we have to pay the tune of about four or five thousand pounds.

We broke the cat down one day, though, using the Purple Phantoms Theatrical Troupe in his office. We gave him a little sobbing routine, and the empty stomach routine, and cracked finger nails, and then we wound up screaming at him.

Jerry: You see, they're only human beings. People get their little vision of the iron-clad gentleman behind his desk in his record company who controls it all. They don't control anything. They're all worried about what the kid on the street is going to buy next. If you go up and scream at those people the results are quite surprising. It really hurts them to think they've gone wrong.

There was no attempt at rational argument. They were no good at that. They tried to do instead what they did with their audience: break them down, convert them, make them part of that constituency that would identify with them as people rather than agree or disagree with them as parties to an argument. The result, believed Jerry, would never really be in doubt. Institutions, routines and roles were, after all, not *real*, and it was no more than the daily business of an agent of transformation like himself to break them down. In the end nothing might be achieved, but that was not how it seemed to the Purple Phantoms. They were unable to evaluate longer-term consequences. All that mattered was the response of the moment, to get a big reaction. They might have sacrificed a few record sales, but at least they had remained loyal to their constituency. They had confirmed its fantasies about the straight world, and acted as the agent of transformation must if the True Believers were not to doubt. At Carraghbay Terrace, Jason and Helen could go on, serving tea to friends.

DRUGS

Why were you dealing?
For the bread. And the excitement.

You mean the illegality of it?
No, just the excitement man, there's a whole thing about being a successful dope dealer. You really do your ego some good. You can be everybody's best friend for quite a little while.

And you just escape with your skin?
Yeah, well that's what happened in the end, yes. Bum

trips, heavy burns, guns, having been busted a dozen times by the law.

Guns, by whom? Competitors, or big organisations, or what?
Greedy people. People you do deals with, you trust them for a while, you do a lot of deals, and low and behold, you've blown it. You know, that fast buck situation. Why not pull a gun on somebody who's come to score 20 grand's worth of dope? Better than walking into a bank and walking out with three or four grand. There's a whole illusion about those long-haired freaks, man. Some of them are really the most evil people you could ever hope to meet. You know what I mean? We do have our criminal element. Perhaps far greater than straight society.

The speaker is a young American who is now part of the entourage of one of the pop groups. He is settled in London, but speaking primarily from recollection of his time as a dealer in drugs in the United States. Such people may no doubt be found many times over in many different localities. He fits an enduring image. The orientation and values are familiar, and transcend most ethnic and cultural barriers: money, excitement, the brief elation of bringing sustenance to the beleaguered, a time-worn combination. He could be drawn with equal facility from contemporary conceptions of Chicago under prohibition, from the days of highwaymen or from the Wild American West: and so, in a sense, he is. Many of the missionaries and traders of the world of drugs are acting out, mainly for audience-effect, the primordial fantasies of straight society in all periods and places.

The popular conception of the role of drugs within hippie groups in the metropolis is no doubt modelled on this archetype. Although some elements may fit, overall it will not do. Apart from everything else, it is undeservedly comforting to straight society and its law-enforcement agencies. It is included as preface to this section to articulate what may be the preconceptions of many readers and which it is important at this point to set aside, if only conditionally.

Drugs are a primary dimension of contemporary youth rebellion and part of the unifying mystique of drop-out groups outside the dominant social order. In the previous chapter, however, I suggested that they should be seen chiefly as a major agency of transformation. It is this possibility I shall now explore. I shall however try to set the process in a wider time-framework, by tracing the whole moral career of a dope-dealer, from his early life, through first initiation to drug use, to full-time engagement and complete financial dependence on dealing. Why did he become a dealer? Why does he continue as one? What does this reveal of the origin and nature of the groups whose economic base and welfare services he partly provides. Such questions cannot of course be isolated from consideration of specific aspects of drug-induced experience: like that of all entrepreneurs, the dope-dealer's commitment is deeply influenced by his perception of the service he is providing.

Rites of passage

For many of the young people who used drugs, it was a temporary stage through which they passed. That must be said even at risk of obscuring the dangers to themselves and problems for others that drug-use may always involve. Probably few began using drugs with the belief that it was something that would be indefinitely sustained. It was often the nature of the initiation and termination of their drug-use that had most significance in their lives, quite beyond the nature of drug-induced experience itself. While some people might be initiated to drug-use quite involuntarily, or with few preconceptions or expectations and only a dim perception of what was happening to them, for many others it undoubtedly had at the time, and even more assumed in retrospect, a special sacramental significance. This was particularly so with the use of LSD. In a society where the transition from adolescence to maturity is marked by few meaningful rites of passage, initiation or graduation in drug-use could be substituted by those within or in contact with drug-using groups. The conception of 'being turned on' itself almost implied transition from one stage of life or mode of existence to another. The ritual of such transformations was given a mystical air: as with all revelations or initiations, it was necessary that the recipient be ready and the moment auspicious:

I turned him on to shit because I thought he had the mentality to take it, to take it where it was, experience it and leave it. (Ben)

I get stoned because I like to understand my mind better. In childhood I couldn't admit myself as I am. I was afraid to stand up as I am. Now I would like to explore myself more, that's why I'm gravitating around these hippies. Very shortly I will be taking some acid. These people who have taken it, they will help me. I've just got to find the right friend. (Elaine)

Listen in particular to Jeremy on this point:

Acid more than any other drug is the sort you have to be ready for. You can't escape into it, because it will frighten you to death, it will frighten you to insanity. Particularly because the people who take acid have usually taken some other sort of drug first. And they know about acid, and they know it will have a very big effect.

First time I used acid, it was a highly significant experience. One of the biggest experiences of one's life, I'd say, for anyone who takes acid.

I had been planning to take acid a long time before I did. I had been offered it for a couple of years. I was planning to take it this June, with friends, back in the States. I regret that I didn't in fact wait. Because I'd say the first trip's the most significant—obviously it must be. They are people I know better and liked better than the people in England.

As with all revelations, in the way Gordon and Annette discussed it, there was a tendency to emphasise how irreversible and absolute were the effects:

Has there been any particular turning point in your life?
Oh definitely, definitely the day I dropped my first acid trip.

For me too.

You've got to take one trip out in a field, away from everything, away from all this man-constructed bullshit, and then you understand what this whole thing is about.

Of those immersed in drug-using groups, such responses were quite typical. A routine question on when LSD was first taken tended to be greeted with responses ranging from mild amusement to derision. About an experience construed as absolute such a question became absurd, a confusion of two dimensions of time, two different universes of discourse and meaning: either before and after were two different people or the latter had obliterated the former. It could be almost a matter of the tiger swallowing its own tail. For many, however, it seemed that in the case of drugs belief in the magic of the commodity and the value of the experience tended to change with time. Revelation did not continue indefinitely. The moment of illumination could not recur. Early or late it might become necessary to move on. To the capacity to see beyond the drug experience there might then attach a similar sense of discovery and illumination, of new awakening rather than re-awakening. Sometimes people found in coming out the same sense of development and personal growth as they had associated with first going in. At one level the young people to whom David, our dealer, would sell drugs would express this by saying that there came a time when there was no more point in taking them. At another they would focus on how it became boring once it became itself a matter of everyday routine: 'Once you've experienced it quite often you get used to its effects and it just becomes a drag like everyday life. You get used to it, so you have a dose of normality and get a buzz from that.'

Nick adopted a somewhat similar position. When his period of transformation was some time passed, and he could look back on the experience with a measure of objectivity and dispassion, he saw the general significance of drugs to transformation, and particularly the importance of initiation and termination of drug-use, in the following way:

Drugs changed my personality, changed my course of life. But I don't know if it was a turning point. If I hadn't taken them, where would I be now? You can always argue the good points and the bad points. A lot of people say you learn a hell of a lot from it, and yet would they learn the same amount in the time if they were not taking drugs?

But it does widen your consciousness, it definitely does, because you're not aware of things, and you become more aware of different things, and you wouldn't experience them if you just remained ordinary. Or I'm pretty sure you wouldn't from the amount of ordinary people you talk to who've never experienced anything like it.

So it must expand—not your consciousness—your feeling. It sort of makes your mind more flexible. To me it's given its advantages and disadvantages in a way. I'm not ashamed to think that I did it.

Because the thing is it's not the actual bad experience really, it's more what you do at the time and the way you think at the time. Life's still the same whether you're taking drugs or not. To so many people nowadays—well to the blokes I know—it's a whole way of life to them, it's their horizon, and they can't think ahead. So all it does is become another little cage. But there's still a window at the end of it, and the thing is if you're aware it's a cage and there's something on the other side, it's all very nice.

But I feel sorry for the people who can't see out of it, they can't see the wood for the trees and they just keep taking—you know really fucking themselves up. I think everyone has got to have this sense to look out from themselves, and when they can't, I'm just praying someone can do something about it.

For the adolescent both entry into and exit from drug-taking might seem such significant moments in their lives that they could precipitate a wider transformation. It was largely on this account that they were endowed with a mystical air and sacramental character.

Why, however, should special significance have been attached to them as an agency of transformation? Why, moreover, should they have had continuing significance in the lives of those young people who used them? To answer this something has to be said, hesitantly, about the nature and effect of the hippie's drug-induced experience. Or, at least, about what they felt to be its nature and effect.

What then was the nature of 'normal' drug-use between the significant moments before and after? Gordon, whom we have already met and who lived by selling drugs, could protest, with some degree of conviction, that it was the job he most wished to be doing, and that done with the right people it gave great satisfaction. We shall see that it was also possible for those at once more experienced and more open and perceptive than him to deem it a calling not without dignity. If the magic was entirely in the beginning and the ending of use, the dealer's occupation would be more uncertain than this, and his commitment less clear. Something about drug-induced experience must have seemed to have value and importance for the young person to engage in what many perceived as a dangerous activity, and for the dealer to be able to provide some measure of self-justification for his activity. Drug-induced experience is obviously highly subjective, so that no single account has much validity, but some general suggestions can be made. The major part of the following account has at least one advantage to commend it: unlike most such accounts, it comes from someone without illusions and with at least a little humour, the dealer whose moral career will be followed in the next section.

New self, new world

If you asked Gordon and David's customers why drug-use had become widespread, they would offer a range of explanations. Even limited investigation can suggest many others. Most of these answers are, however, too far removed from the actual experience itself to carry much conviction. Most seem little more than pre-conditions or contributory causes. Ultimately the dominant and overriding reason must be sought in the nature of drug-induced experience itself.

This is not to say that these contributory causes are not important. It is obviously important that middle-class children receive large amounts of pocket money, and that 'there's nothing else to spend it on that's really important'. But why are drugs important? Maybe drug-use is 'much more fun' because it is illegal, but why is it fun in the first place? Perhaps one reason it spreads is that 'there's not much point in doing it alone', but what is special about doing it with others? It is certainly part of the importance of drugs to young people that it is one subject on which they are vastly more knowledgeable than their parents and so for once have the advantage, but this alone is hardly likely to be the critical factor.

The young customers themselves would all offer such explanations as these. Many had read A-level sociology and knew roughly what was acceptable as a reason or would pass as a cause. When they discussed the question more discursively, however, they always returned to the effects of drugs in terms which suggested these were the real reasons for taking them. 'Black Bombers', one would remark, 'keep you awake all night.' 'When you take Mandrax', another would add, 'and you touch something, your whole body tingles.' It is diverting to recall that this very tingling sensation was what made listening to Strauss Mrs Adams's favourite leisure-time pursuit. Before the mists of doubt descend upon Strauss's reputation, it should perhaps be added that people respond to stimuli in different ways, and some people—so my informants claimed—had even been known to get a buzz from staring at a blank wall.

In Norman Zinberg's terminology (1967), drug-users divided into two categories, the oblivion-seekers and the experience-seekers. David, our dealer, fell unequivocally into the second category, as his reaction to heroin, the archetypal oblivion drug, had demonstrated:

Junkies are all invalids of one sort or another. I went through the junk thing two years ago. I felt it was groovy to stick needles in myself. Didn't last long and I never took large quantities.

Heroin I found very boring. It's very, very comforting if you're unhappy. If you're one of those people who is congenitally unhappy, it's the ideal thing because it solves every problem in a flash, and makes you feel very good—gives you security, a sense of well-being, gives you a place to look out from, builds a little warm house around you. But as you come down the little warm house dissolves and the wind blows through, so the natural thing to do is just to take some more. But it takes three weeks to become an addict, and going at it quite hard, you know. You have to take some every day. It always used to make me feel shitty the next day, and the last thing I wanted to do was to take more. I never went through the experience

of feeling good again, because by the time the next day
came I could see the reason I felt shitty. I never understood
how these people who do take more in order to stop feeling
shitty got around to it because I could never get around
to it. Also I'm naturally optimistic, you know, it was just
a morbid little dallying.

We have seen that for a high proportion of those outside
the dominant social order, their position there was the result
less of choice than of personal disaster of one kind or another.
For them the search for oblivion ended in the kind of experience
David described. The opiates brought a utopia of a sort, brief
and tragic, but it was not the kind in which David primarily
traded. He sold the experience-augmenting drugs—besides
cannabis, the amphetamines and the psychedelic drugs—whose
effects were quite different. For all that David was, as we shall
see, relatively old and cynical and bereft of illusions, he did
still believe that drugs could intensify experience: they could
give you a feeling of importance, take you out of your strict
limitations, make the world seem beautiful and the self feel
intense:

A lot of drugs give you an enormous feeling of self-
importance, particularly amphetamine. It has the most
extraordinary effect on you, really weird. They give you the
most enormous feeling of importance and destiny, if you
see what I mean. Acid has a similar effect—not self-
importance, but self-worth. You can write dreadful poems
and find them marvellous under acid.

Mainly I think acid loosens you up a little, if you know
what I mean. It shows you a very definite other way of
thinking, of looking at things, and proves that there are
many more. And therefore lifts you out of your strict
upbringing. And even if you can't think outside them,
it shows you that there is one other way of thinking at
least—and so it gives you another place to start from.

But apart from that, I don't think it does much for you.
And once you've done it once, or a few times, you've
passed that and I think it's a bit of a waste of time.

I trip very seldom now. I did take some mescalin recently
which was very nice, very enjoyable. But I don't approve of

chemicals, part of my same sentimentalism about the twentieth century. This mescalin was synthetic. I took it sitting in a wood. It turned into a sort of disneyland wood, the colours were sort of separated, if you see what I mean—the tree trunk was sort of separated into the component colours that made up the colour that it was. Really very attractive and beautiful. It made you laugh a lot, with no heavy philosophical problems which is always what I disliked about acid—you know, finding yourself feeling all intense.

Finally, cannabis itself. As the 'recreational drug of choice' among some groups not easily designated deviant, it was acquiring a general importance which is not our concern. What was its specific importance to hip outsiders, among whom its use was ubiquitous? David was clear and categorical: 'The smoke stops the tedium—the one great attribute of hash, it makes you sit around in your pad and do nothing and enjoy every minute of it.'

After this brief inventory of goods, let us meet the dealer.

The moral career of a dope-dealer

David was ultimately traced for interview by a combination of accident and duplicity. Nothing had come of a long series of messages and attempted meetings at the affluent parental home near Wimbledon Common. In the hippie world of Ladbroke Grove, to which he had long since seceded, he was equally elusive. This evening it was different, a fair cop. He was mildly surprised, not enough to dent the charm: he had not really been avoiding me, he had just received the messages at times he was sure it would have been inconvenient and thoughtless to 'phone. And those weeks in Wales had been an act of desperation after a long dirty winter in the city, 'and because I thought it a reasonable sort of thing to do to put 230 miles between me and my parents for a while'. Self-confident and at ease, he showed no hint of the contrived and highly-strung relaxation which is so often the social anaesthetic of outsiders. Perhaps this was because he was caught by surprise, perhaps because he was too old and experienced, perhaps because of a certain arrogance. In these and other ways he was probably not typical of the entrepreneurs of the drug world, though his background may well have been similar to many, and his career in drugs was certainly similar to most.

He was in good humour: there were signs that his parents had at last begun to give him up. He was getting on better with them. To any suggestion that they were interesting and admirable people he would make no response. But he did worry about them: he felt responsibility to them to the extent that their happiness was, among other things, a responsibility of his; and he knew he made them unhappy. They were, he said, 'Puritanical in a socialist sort of way, with an enormous capacity for disapproval. They disapprove of entrepreneuring— private medicine, let alone illicit drugs: strong Fabian principles.' His father was to David's friends a source of endless confusion; he seemed a drop-out with social responsibility, to whom doing his own thing had been establishing a formidable career by a most unconventional route. Not only had he managed to raise two families, he had also contrived to fight in both World Wars. David himself, after a succession of girl-friends he in retrospect considered rather weird, was now settled with Georgina, although it was never quite clear how far his devotion was the result of her having once been dubbed by his parents with the accolade of being 'as hopeless as he is'. It was said that some women were struck by David's lack of animal cunning: others by his resemblance to his father.

He spent all his time reading, except for such spasms of activity arranging drug deals as market conditions allowed and his pocket dictated. After eighteen months of dealing he was now feeling somewhat discontented. He was therefore in reflective mood, and went back to the beginning.

I was at a vaguely progressive public school. I was far too bloody frightened at the time to enjoy it, quite paranoid. School-children set on outcasts, and I was always a bit of an outcast. Although reputedly intelligent I made repeated and consistent failures of everything I turned my hand to.

Well, I didn't really turn my hand to anything at all, except sit on my arse all day. I didn't fit into any of the roles that are asked of one at a prep school or a public school. Teachers used to get very annoyed with me because I would act in a seemingly intelligent manner in class, and would hand in the most God-awful shit for homework. I used to get 'bone idle, that's what you are bone idle'. It was quite true. I was once beaten for being bad at mathematics: 'persistently bad at mathematics'.

In order to shut out the outside world I used to read all the time. I was a boarder, from the age of nine to 16. I objected to the idea, and demanded that I be released from it. So I was sent to a psychoanalyst. My parents thought it was a good idea. I was sent to a string of them with no effect. I used one of these psychoanalysts to persuade them that the best thing would be for me to leave school entirely and go to a college in London to take my A-levels.

In his unwillingness or incapacity to fulfil the roles and expectations of the school community lay the obvious origins of his subsequent alienation from the wider social order. Being isolated and outcast in this way could no doubt predispose the individual to a generalised rejection of the social order, and to rebellion when opportunity presented itself. It would be wrong to presume, however, that such opportunity was deliberately and consciously seized. This time the actor stumbled almost fortuitously into his role, and then could not see his way out of it: he had therefore to revise his conception of the social order and his relations with it to fit the new perspective from which he had to view it. It was in this way that the dominant social order could be rationalised by people like David as the 'system', a set of formal, empty and exclusive relationships, closed to energy and activity from him and open only to information about him. Although, as we shall see, David had moved somewhat into this way of accounting for himself, he was too honest and intelligent to propagate it with conviction. The trouble had been in him, not in his stars. Society demanded of its members a degree of involvement and commitment, and those too arrogant or shy to give it were inevitably outcast. David saw the trouble.

I can never get right into anything really. I'm too detached. I've got something vaguely out of a Dostoevsky novel attitude, sort of thinking that I don't like being too involved in anything, that it's not really very good form, you know. I don't know what sort of a novel would fit such a character.

Detachment could be lonely, uncomfortable and stressful. The outsider would in most cases come sooner or later upon relationships which provided some measure of warmth, identification and relief:

Having been at College for three weeks someone turned me on. From then on, I suddenly found myself in a position in which I could feel at home. I was only 16 or 17, impressionable and all that. And I was impressed by this section of society and attempted to become one. Not that I think of myself as one now—I have gone through that sort of self-conscious attempt at it.

It was a moment of transformation of a sort, a feeling more particularly of coming in from the cold. David was too well balanced and self-aware to construe it as much more. Why then was he attracted? To ask that is to ask why he could identify with such an outsider group when he felt only detachment from the dominant society and its ways.

I don't know. I suppose because the standard world that was offered seemed rather tedious. And also I didn't have any of the qualifications to get me any job that was any good. I did three years of interminable boredom, which again I was doing to satisfy my parents—their thinking I could work my way up to a good job—and eventually I just chucked it up.

Graduation from being a member of a drug-using group to making a living from trading drugs followed an essentially similar pattern. It was a casual and pragmatic act, to which he was predisposed by a fundamentally similar constellation of personal factors:

I was out of work, and I knew someone who could provide substance A and I knew someone who wanted it and I just put two and two together. I didn't have any money and suddenly ended up with more money than I ever had before. It wasn't a conscious decision. I make very few conscious decisions. I think that's the only reason why I am in this position, because I can't make decisions, because I can't see what is better than what. You need some sort of a position from which to make a conscious decision, some sort of role, some sort of a little platform, from which you feel you can judge up a situation, and I didn't feel that I had it.

But there was something more than that:

I've also got this thing about people's dignity. It seems to me that really very few people could be called dignified. I think that being a dealer is being more dignified than being a clerk. Do you see what I mean? I don't know really, but I did years of clerkship and got shouted at by lots of horrible men. Maybe it's arrogant of me.

To an extent David had a conventional belief in roles, status, order, responsibility, but it was overlaid by an essentially romantic belief in innocence and autonomy. It was here perhaps that the roots of detachment lay: the standard world and conventional occupations within it seemed, by his standards, cheap and undignified. If innocence and autonomy were not to be betrayed, to be a dealer was a solution. David was aware it was only one among the possibilities. His sister 'looks after junkies', working at the kind of clinic to which Sue might have found her way, a contrast which did not go unnoticed. The inevitable satirical comment could not cloak the serious implications:

I make them, she breaks them! I suppose doing that sort of thing is just her interpretation of the same problem, and that she doesn't just want to become part of someone else's money-making machine. Her answer is to do something like that. My answer is to become my own money-making machine, which is perhaps not quite so upright.

Such a clinical attitude to his calling was not entirely in character, even though he drifted almost fortuitously into it. Aside from the warmth and identification his sub-culture provided, the moral implications of his activities were the subject of an appropriate and increasing hesitation:

When I was at College, I was quite a rarity—there were maybe three in my class. Now all the freshly scrubbed young ones tumbling out of school, or all the ones I've met, are latent dope-smokers. Customers! What worries me is that they haven't got the doubts that I've got. I've always been pretty doubt-ridden.

Why, once initiated in dealing, had he then continued over the eighteen months? How had his attitudes changed during that period? Why did he now feel a certain discontent? The answers were inextricably entwined, and perceptible only in a full account of what those eighteen months had involved, and in particular of what the role of dealer might involve.

While I was at school, in order to shut out the outside world, I used to read all the time, and the only thing I could ever get into was literature. So I thought this was the thing to do: I worked in two bookshops, a library and two publishing firms. Then I chucked it in and became a forklift truck driver, which was much more fun. It was really quite nice. It was at this brewery, built in 1785. We'd steal beer, smoke joints around the back of the tanks, and roar around driving these trucks. It was really quite amusing and I was making more money than anywhere else. Then I got chucked out, because we used to have to start at 7, and I never used to get to bed before 1 or 2, and so sometimes I didn't make it. Then they told me if I didn't make it again don't come back. I woke up at 11.30 that morning. Shortly after that someone said, psst, I've got some grass. So I found myself in a position to make some money in a different way—well, by being an entrepreneur, which is all I am or ever will be. Never actually doing anything myself, just arranging little deals. It made me much more money than I was ever able to make any other way. It was more interesting, sort of varied outdoor life. Your own master and all that. It wasn't very dangerous. It's getting more dangerous now. You see, I only arrange deals that involve large quantities, sort of 20 pounds or 30 pounds, generally for export to America, because there is a lot of money in it and I put a commission on whatever I arrange or do.

It's quite exciting, and you have to play people off against each other, and get good prices. It takes a degree of skill and organisation, and tact, and subtlety and how to get things right. And there's the awful problem that A has some money and B has some shit. A mustn't meet B, and A doesn't want to let go of his bread and B doesn't want to let go of his shit. Basic problem. One generally works it somehow. A and B have to retain their status. So it becomes quite like a game at some times. If it goes well, it's very satisfying. If it goes badly, it's really depressing. It's more fun than any job I could get, as regards funny.

Last year the number of dealers in London was quite small, and they all knew each other and there was a big atmosphere and camaraderie. Now there are many, many more people just catching on to it as a way of living without working.

It is getting much more dangerous. Last year the fuzz were really incredibly naïve. This year, they're not. It doesn't much improve their efficiency at being able to bust you, because the whole thing is blessedly erratic. It has no organisation. It's a whole load of amateurs. But it's getting so damn dangerous, that it's really getting not worth it. The returns are getting smaller and smaller, because of the competition. There's a greater demand than supply, much greater now, much more than last year. Last year you could roam about doing smaller quantities. Now you have to be fast to get there on time. Someone comes in with a pile, and like you've got to be there on the day, or else you miss out, and it's all gone.

Almost like being up at seven again, and jockeying for position, keeping everybody in touch, reminding the fellow that you want so many, and making sure that the fellow is there waiting.

I can see that it can only end one way, and I don't want it to end that way. I am also getting a little dissatisfied with the returns, quite honestly, for the amount of effort put into it. And also it's an unsettled life. You work every day, although you don't seem to do anything at all. And it's hot and harassing and the money's not regular. You can never be sure of any, which is a bit depressing sometimes, if you've got 2p in your pocket. And as it gets more and more difficult, so there are more and more people around with no money in their pockets, and so there are more and more prepared to be nasty. Get a break, man, lift some money and take off. They're always so short-sighted because they can't see that the only place they've got to come is back.

It does give one a certain sense of importance and responsibility. You handle quite large quantities of money and that sort of thing. A Real Man you know? Not a phoney, not a plastic replica, but the real thing.

And at first the danger was a big thrill. Now I'm getting bored with it. And I don't want to go to prison. I also felt I was serving some sort of purpose and all that. Difficult to put into words. I don't feel that so much now. It all seemed rather romantic. I felt quite heroic. The quality of hash has gone down, a lot, since more money-obsessed people got in on the act. Now it's beginning to strike people that there's more things to living than hustling dope. Getting more wide boys in the game, still essentially hippie wide boys, but wide boys.

There was a report in the Sunday Express about this time last year, entitled 'The Pusher'—the picture of this guy was of someone with a shiny car, a mohair suit and fat cigar, and quoting lots of arbitrary figures like 'the pusher makes £15,000 a year!' You know it was all sort of 'Out of the degradation of our youth' and that sort of crap. I am constantly astounded by the crassness and naïveté of the daily press. I mean they have really no idea. I really ought to have written off to them and told them where it's at: I'm a dealer, I haven't got no £7,000 car, only a beat-up motor cycle. They've all been seeing too many Edgar Wallace movies.

Death of a salesman

David started just doing little things for friends, and graduated subsequently to more substantial operations. He stumbled into it. He did not will himself to become a dealer. What kept him doing it was the excitement and danger and the exercise of a degree of skill and finesse. More important, however, was the fact that the dealer performed an essential role within the hip sub-culture. David consequently had, to begin with, a certain sense of vocation—'a feeling that I was performing some sort of purpose and all that'. This derived from his own transformation, and the belief that there must be something worth while in communicating it. The drug-using sub-culture had provided him with a sense of identity, a feeling of being 'at home' which he had not previously felt, and a belief that certain of his drug experiences had been valuable to someone confronting a dreary and uninviting world.

Now something had gone wrong, in fact two things. Of one David was aware. It echoed back to his evaluation of drug-induced experience itself: it changed with time. It gave you, he still maintained, another place to start from, and its importance in transformation remained, but he had discovered that more general values did not endure. If you had used drugs once or a few times, he now saw, they became a bit of a waste of time.

This was critically important; entrepreneurial roles in the hippie world were distinguished by the fact that they were total. It was the same for David as for Phil and Jerry and Doug: what we do is what we live. Without personal belief and involvement there was nothing. If his own belief in and commitment to the transcendent value of drug-use changed, the dealer's role had to end, or at least change equally dramatically. The one was dependent on the other. It could never be just a job.

The second change was intimately linked to the first. David revealed it in the way he now described the world of dealing. Originally there was a sense of magic and mission, an opportunity to be someone and do something. What may have been, from some points of view, an essentially sordid exercise was bathed in a glow of romantic nobility. By comparison with the apparently dreary possibilities of the standard world, the drug-using sub-culture had been some sort of utopia, and drug-dealing a romantic mission, at least by comparison with being a clerk. That had all changed. The quality of hash was going down. Professional standards were declining. People were getting obsessed with money, so that the transcendental purposes were becoming lost from view. All this was probably partly true. Over the course of eighteen months such developments may have been in some measure taking place. These factors, however, were hardly likely to have been more than a small part of the explanation of the change in his attitudes. More probably, the changed perception of the world of drug-dealing grew directly from the change in David's perception and valuation of drug experience itself. Roles and missions required belief to sustain them in a way that mere jobs did not.

There was also something else at work which changed the character of the dealer's role and commitment. The drug-dealer was one of the people who mediated between the different realities of hip and straight but, much more than underground musicians or any of the others, he was liable progressively to be torn apart by the conflicting values of their different worlds. Within hippie communities he might never have quite the charismatic power of the musician, but the dealer's contribution to its sacramental, economic and welfare functions was even more critical than theirs. Moreover, as we have heard one informant remarking already, he could be everyone's friend for quite some little while. Had he been able to spend all his time in the sub-culture, everything would have been well. But he could not. He had to go foraging into the straight world, and the fact that his role and activities were proscribed and damned there immediately raised problems. It was not just the police and the fear of imprisonment. He could never relax his wariness or be unthinkingly trusting; one kind of crime forced him inevitably into contact with other sorts of crime and other kinds of criminals, with deceit and theft and violence. What was sacramental ritual in one context was sordid racketeering in another. Knowledge of the latter had at some point to undermine belief in the former: the two could not be completely separated. The dope-dealer had to live with the conflict: unlike the pop group, he could not simply howl at a manager or tear up a contract. The role was perhaps too demanding for anyone to stay in it long. The dealer might not accept straight society's attitudes towards drugs, but he still could not avoid their consequences.

In particular, the straight world did, unwittingly, one rather terrible thing to people like David. The fact that cannabis, LSD and the rest were illegal raised their value and their price.

In the long term this emphasised the explicitly commercial nature of the transactions in which they were involved. Ironically it was this very commercial world from which most dealers originally dropped out to become hippies. The dealer might be *his own* moneymaking machine, but, as the straight world would not allow him for one moment to forget, he was a money making machine none the less. It was this realisation that in the long run destroyed the original sense of mission.

What of David himself? When last seen he was still dealing. When most other beliefs about it had vanished, he at least still found it more fun, 'in the sense of funny', than such other things as were open.

What was different was that a more conventional identity, which had been falteringly evolving in the years since the effects of transformation began to wane, had reached some fulfilment, though it had done so in a paradoxical way:

> I have at last found my own character and I don't have to use other people's. At one time I was playing the joker all the time, and it was because I really didn't have anything else. I had to build one up. The whole thing came to an end at the end of a long saga of drugs, when I sort of whacked my mind completely. I became desperately confused characterwise, if you see what I mean, because I didn't really have a personality, so I used to make up personalities. The personalities got very confused, and I didn't know what was going on, and I took too much methedrine for a while, and that'll wipe anything out, and then I sort of lost my mind for a while. I took a long rest, and came back with a new one, freshly ironed (*laughter*). Been much more together since then. I don't feel like a hippie at all. I feel like me. I feel like the same me that I was before but I could never feel it.

Whether this new identity had come because of or in spite of his experiences in the world of drugs, and whether it could really endure, are unanswerable questions. All that is clear is that David had become The Survivor. He would acknowledge that he had been among the lucky ones. It may have been his natural optimism that had prevented him finishing up as one of the 'bombed-out freaks, tragedies of the hippie world' whom he met at every turn. More probably it was that very detachment, that inability to get 'right into things' which had, paradoxically, entailed his original estrangement from the dominant social order and his entry into the drug world. It allowed him to go through transformation, and the commitment and enthusiasm that followed it, without the involvement ever being quite *total*. There was always the possibility of moving on if experience dictated.

The detachment had been destructive in adolescence. It might be less so now. David would probably take the opportunity to return to the straight world, if one presented itself. But this remained his problem. Though he had changed, the world had not. He may simply have learnt better how to survive within it, alienated and alone, the missionary without a calling.

> The prospects are rapidly rushing up on me. Here's me, 23 years old, and with not much experience at anything, except a lot of office work. And I can't really carry on dealing, because that's no way to live. And I don't know what to do.

FESTIVAL

The way of life described in the second chapter continued with hardly a break. But for a few days of the summer the area of Ladbroke Grove and Notting Hill Gate where Maggie, Elaine, Gordon and the rest were settled would seem strangely deserted. Federalearth Freaks and the Purple Phantoms would be silent, and between eleven at night and seven in the morning no noctambulists would disturb the hours of rest of the straight people, something even more strange to them than the temporary reassertion of their lost dominion which the day allowed. A Pop Festival weekend: when the sun came out in summer, the long-haired people had somewhere to go, whereas in winter they were homeless or hibernating. Just as Ladbroke Grove was left to the straights, so the West End was left to the tourists. Sue would make a brief sortie on each of the festivals; Jimmy would go down in the clean clothes normally reserved for visits to his mother, and Ben found there the chance to sleep in the open undisturbed by the police, as the previous summer he had been able to do in the London parks. For a while the moral unity of all who appear in this book became an identity of time and space. We take leave of them lost for once in the same crowd, but not without discovering how and why they were there, for, trite and commercial as the pop festival may have become, we shall see that it could still function to provide periodic affirmation of the culture described in these pages and a kind of communal expurgation of some of the doubts and apprehensions underlying it.

Like drugs and pop music, festivals functioned to preserve and renew hip culture. They were, however, different in other ways. Because they were occasional and special, their part in the hippie's life was less fundamental and integral than that of drugs and pop music. Festivals were also secondary to drugs and music because drugs and music were themselves such a large part of a festival. To some extent festivals may have been simply vehicles, providing an environment congenial to the primary interest focused on drugs and music. Moreover, because festivals were generally substantial commercial operations, the entrepreneurs who conceived and guided them were often not part of the hippie sub-culture, in the way the pop groups and the drug-dealers often were. Festivals are nevertheless important in any account of how hippie culture was preserved and renewed.

The evolution of a ritual

How and why did they begin? What was it about them that made them survive and develop? On their origins, I can do no more than relay to the reader the word of Neil and Ray, two of my sample who had been present at the creation and centrally involved in subsequent developments. In historical perspective they saw two particular lines of development. One grew out of the Marquee Festival of the National Jazz Federation, but was given impetus more particularly by a new kind of benefit concert, 'The Fourteen Hour Technicolour Dream', arranged by a number of people connected with *I.T.*, the underground newspaper. Music here was the starting-point, but no more.

There had been concerts before, but what was fundamentally different about the Fourteen Hour Technicolour Dream was the time-scale enshrined in its title, and which was to find a culmination at Woodstock, expressed so crisply in the record of the festival: 'Three whole days, man.' The importance of the time factor perhaps found some confirmation also in what Neil regarded as another source of the tradition: the Aldermaston Marches. If there was one common historical experience that had marked the development of the people represented in these pages, it was this. Its importance resided partly in the time factor, but also in the bringing together over time of large numbers of people in an unstructured social setting.

Time was important because it was necessary for the breaking-down of the inhibitions and rigidities of the personality and for the building-up of a sense of fantasy and enthusiasm which would give the festival a life of its own outside the normal world surrounding it. If this was one critical element the other was numbers, something enjoyed on an Aldermaston March as much as at a pop festival. Aldermaston was among the first of what were to be called 'be-ins'. It was from these that festivals derived, and it was the number of people and the atmosphere of the occasion, rather than the music that was crucial.

> I think it used to be just the Festival itself, rather than the music that brought people. Like Aldermaston. I think that had a lot to do with it. Where you get 50, or a 100, or 200,000 people, young people, together, and you really used to groove on it. It was a gas. But there are so many Festivals now—you didn't have to pay for Aldermaston, either.

Not all 'be-ins' were as structured as Aldermaston. Equally important, according to Ray at least, was another line of development. This consisted in smaller and relatively spontaneous gatherings of people. Here again however, they became fairly rapidly gatherings of significant numbers of people.

> Bath and the ones which have already happened and are about to happen grew out of spontaneous gatherings of people, which started from about '66–7. We would take guitars on to Hampstead Heath, play a little bit, sing a little bit; there would be more people of similar inclination who would gather round. We would have what was then

called a be-in. Somebody said what a good idea if we have an electric group. So there was an electric group or two, and a free concert or two here and there and they grew into the big free concerts in Hyde Park.

What these comments implied was that the critical ingredients of success were time and numbers. If festivals were partly vehicles for drugs and music, they were even more important for the numbers of people involved and the period of time over which they took place. The quality of the music, to begin with often poor, and either deafening or inaudible, might in itself lead one to suspect this. There was also the fact that hundreds of young people would stay on long after the end of each festival; at one notable instance in Powder Ridge, Connecticut, more than 30,000 people arrived for and stayed through a festival from which all music had been banned.[1]

What was it about sheer numbers that was important? In part it may have been the transcendence of loneliness and the feeling—of which the outsider is normally deprived—of solidarity. Ray set this in historical perspective:

People go to be a part of it. It's a demonstration of strength really, when 300,000 go somewhere. There used to be insane calls like 'there will be a mass demonstration outside the gates of Buckingham Palace at 2 p.m. on Friday afternoon—just to see how many we could get in those days.

People who go are probably no more lonely than other people. But feel to be—I feel to be—apart from straight society. 'Hey man, there are a lot of freaks around', we'd be saying a few years back, 'let's all get together.'

Once at the club we announced that everyone should meet at Battersea Park at 3 o'clock the following day. It was a joke, but we did happen to be going, so we said it and thought how nice if other people came along, just for a loon. And 200 people turned up. And all 200 of us just spent the entire day just going round the Park. It's just nice to be together, it's nice to be able to just talk to people you've never even seen before. You don't know them and you may never even see them again, but it doesn't matter: we have that much in common. We know we have hash and acid, or music or whatever, but that is just a key.

Also the crowd increased the possibility of losing the self and dissolving the personality.

There were here the key ingredients that, as described in Chapter 3, characteristically induced and sustained the process of transformation. The drawing out of time could dissolve identity by breaking the routines and habits of the everyday personality. The extension of time meant also that the period could take on the characteristic analogy of the journey or searching for the new self. The overwhelming weight of numbers was there to provide a new plausibility and such moral support as adoption of a new life might require. Finally, the concentration on a single event and mode of existence, and its isolation from any other reality, worked to build-up that sense of magic and fantasy, that heightened experience of mind and body, which could be the key and precipitating element of transformation.

This does not mean that pop festivals did effect some transformation in large numbers of young people, though they may have done so. But they provided periodic opportunities for the acting out and repetition of the previous transformations which most of my subjects had experienced and which mediated their original entry into the world of the hip outsider. Essentially a pop festival was sacred drama—the collective re-enactment of the archetypal event in the career of the hip outsider.

The sacraments of renewal

This periodic process of de-socialisation—the breaking-down of the 'personality' which even temporary existence within conventional society tended inevitably to reproduce—permitted the reconsolidation of those modes of experience to which hippies have become committed. To see how this happened we shall listen to the reactions to the festival of three of the people whose attitudes and experiences we have already dwelt upon: first Elaine whom it will be recalled had not gone through any full transformation in my sense of the word; second, Nick whose transformation we have dwelt upon most fully; and finally, David, the old and disillusioned drug-dealer whose transformation took place long in the past. Let me first, however, make some general observations, which may help lend some credence to my thesis, on the manner in which festivals were perceived and described by hippies.

These preliminary observations are drawn primarily from reports of festivals appearing in the 'underground' press, the newspapers and journals that most fully represented the hippie constituency. These reports were generally couched within the philosophy of extremity, and there was often a mystical or millennial ring about them, going beyond normal journalistic hyperbole: 'Isle of Wight—the last great festival', proclaimed the published record of that event: 'Atlanta; the biggest—and maybe last?', reads the magazine *Rolling Stone* of August 1970. Such reports represented a persistent theme. By the same token, it was always reported that the promoters had lost a fortune and they also always proclaimed that such a monumental event could never be tried again. As it turned out, they seldom seemed to have lost much money, if any, and invariably they did repeat the experience. There was the same imagery of the ultimate and the absolute, of death and rebirth, as was used to describe individual transformation. They had almost the same underlying structure as the major acts of celebration that characterised archaic societies: the destruction of an old and guilt-laden world, and the rebirth of a new. (See Mircea Eliade, 1954.) It may be, indeed, that they fulfilled a similar function. Hippie society was like the archaic societies, at least as Mircea Eliade described them, in that it did not have that large element of routine and short-term repetition which is suposed to be a psychological mode of repression and a way of handling guilt. In archaic societies guilt, it was said, was customarily expunged by periodic festivals whose major ritual embodied destruction and rebirth. Whether or not such connection is there, festivals often seemed to fill a similar role.

The reports of festivals also placed emphasis on spontaneity and surprise. They were described in the same ways as Phil or Doug would describe the structure of their concerts. There was an unpredictable moment of transformation, when individuals were made to break out of their defensive shells, and the event suddenly came alive. Characteristic of such moments were the rain storm at Woodstock and the fire on stage at the Isle of Wight. I do not know whether such an accident has characterised all successful festivals, but I suspect it may have.

The reader may recall Jerry's remark that people wanted to get back to the earth, so the very fact that these two particular accidents involved the elements—here fire and water—may possibly have added another element of significance to them. These, however, can be no more than the vaguest speculations. Let me return, then, to the experiences of people in the study.

The reader will recall that Elaine had gone through one stage of transformation—the breakdown and disintegration of old values—without coming upon the other—the plausibility structure for a new self and a new life. When she went to the festival for the first time, it was to discover what essentially it was like. It was also to aid that transformation process; to help lose an old, disintegrated self, felt to be inadequate, and to hear the call of a new life. The reader should note again the symbolism of the elements.

I went to see what a festival is. I've never been to one before. And then I very much like pop music. And I wanted as well to be lost in everything. I mean everybody. And the best way to do it is just to crawl within a crowd.

There were some people who didn't like the crowd, and who built up some tents, and were listening to the music from far away. It was something I couldn't understand. They probably came for the music; they didn't come for the people. I came for both. The idea of community: we were all sitting in the mud. We didn't mind about the mud. We were very close to the earth. It started to rain, and we were just like a tree. Like a big bush. A big bush of people. Waiting for the sounds. Of life. We were a big tree with lots of branches, and every one of us were leaves. Some were trunk. Some were branches. I was probably just a little leaf.

It's very important. A tree wouldn't live without leaves, otherwise it would be just a dead tree. It enabled me to be myself. I could jump up and do whatever I wanted to do. I could smoke, I could dance, I could jump, and freak out. I like to freak out. I walked in without paying. So I tricked. I cheated. And I enjoyed that.

Probably few of those attending the festival saw it in quite the way Elaine did. A large proportion were, in a sense, hangers-on, holiday-makers and tourists numbered among that large section of conventional youth who had absorbed certain 'hip' forms of dress and leisure activity without adopting their full life-style. If these constituted the majority, the next largest group was not of novitiates like Elaine but of true believers like Nick.

Nick was settled. He expected from the festival no new dawn of self-discovery. The scales had already fallen from his eyes. He was already among the enlightened. In his mind there was little doubt about the rightness of the life pursued since his transformation. If there was no new dawn, the reaffirmation of transformation which the pop festival allowed was not without its own joy. For Nick its significance was clear and it was that general significance I have suggested: the pop festival 'breaks down your personality'—that straitjacket which mere existence within society little by little enforced upon one. At the festival one went through, in modified and attenuated form, the dissolution of the old self and rediscovery of the new. It was in this sense above all that the festival had some element of sacred ritual, for one aspect of ritual is the dissolution of individual identity within a larger and purer collectivity.[2]

As with transformation, so with re-enactment. It was other people who formed the crucial mediating factor, the key element in the plausibility structure:

> For me it's the people first. A nice bunch of people with the same ideas, and everybody's so happy because they're all sort of together. You don't get the same sort of togetherness in a football crowd or anything like that. It's amazing. Nothing like this has happened except religious meetings where everyone does have the same ideas, but there's nothing sort of religious in it, which is one of the interesting things. And there's very little violence or anything like that.

Nick was the devotee. And when the devotee re-enacted sacred ritual he did it with joy and happiness, but also with a humility and self-abasement. Beholding Nick and his fellow devotees, Neil, the entrepreneur of the new society, saw all this:

Down there the standard of living was pretty appalling, but everyone was having quite a good time—I mean such a good time that they had to get 100 cops in to throw them out eventually because they were really enjoying themselves. They had to walk quarter of a mile to get their water and that in terms of a standard of living was pretty terrible, but they were happier there than they were in the Grove, where not only did the water come through the pipe, but the sewage went out through the pipe, but that was about it. It was the lowest level of existence, right, but they seemed happy enough.

No doubt even for the hard-core devotees, living in the mud and making homes from twigs and branches, the festival was great fun. The extremity of experience was valued partly for its *extremity*, but partly perhaps also because it would be seen as a ritual cleansing, from which the individual would emerge purified and strengthened.

As for David, he had experienced his transformation many years before, and, as we saw, his sense of calling was now long passed, far beyond anything the re-enactment of sacred ritual could evoke. He went to the festival, with the sense that it was a thing to be done. He gazed in amazement at the world created for themselves by those now following the path he long ago trod, the 'freshly scrubbed young ones, all latent dope-smokers', seemingly now a whole generation in place of the rarities that he and his contemporaries had been. He felt himself the outsider to a movement that had gone beyond him. So far as transformation was concerned, he had been through it all before. When the possibility appeared of a new transformation or even of that renewal of the old which Nick still so much welcomed, he walked firmly on. He never really entered the festival. The time of transformation long passed, he had to gaze on it from the outside:

A lot of them seemed to be playing little 'surviving in the wild' games. Just like bullocks, pretending to fawn each other, doing all this sort of running about. I think it is an instinctive sort of thing, hardly even conscious. I don't think they think of it as fantasy. I think it is an end in itself for them.

Very strange. They all made little homes, hundreds of people, grouped together, sitting in piles of rubbish all over a field, windswept, a little bit of rain, rather chilly, all huddled and sleeping. All very strange. They go out of their way to suffer the most extraordinary degradations.

An enormous number of people, and really like there was 250,000 people, anyway quite a lot, and all of them pretending that everyone else wasn't there. It was incredibly cool. All these people, making little homes. It was really rather like the end of the world—lots of people sitting around on an empty bit of land, burning rubbish fires, with empty coke tins all around them, and sitting there with glazed expressions in their eyes.

I was bombed out of my head for the whole festival. I smoked an ounce of dope all by myself. In two days. I just sort of wandered around, I could never sit down. Ooh, no! I thought that if I sat down I might sort of run into it, and get swallowed up, and never get up again. But if I walked around, I'd be okay.

Anyone who has sat through a pop festival will recognise the accuracy of David's description, particularly of the indulgence of pure animal playfulness. 'Only the animal is truly innocent', wrote Hegel, and the periodic ritual of the festival was an attempt to return to the innocence of original transformation. It was an attempt to return to mythical 'pure' time, the time of the 'instant' of transformation. The transcendence of conventional historical time was possible only in those extreme experiences that fused mind and body, which took the individual 'out of himself', dissolved his personality and allowed him simply to live for the moment. That, at least, was the goal of these periodic re-creations. The extremity of these strange events, in noise, in numbers, in time, drama and the rituals of togetherness, testified to the importance attached to such periodic regeneration.

For the majority it was probably enough. They could return to their homelands, having experienced the salvation, and be sustained through a winter homeless or hibernating. Among our people, David, alone, was too old and too tired.

VI

DECAY

All this poses a familiar question. Did the behaviour and values that have been described represent just a 'stage' through which the young people would pass when some magical combination of external circumstances and internal processes of development decreed that the moment was ripe? Or did they in some sense represent a stable identity which could remain indefinitely? The question follows almost automatically from the particular configurations of beliefs and behaviour which marked my informants, for the reader who hears Jimmy and Sue, David and Maggie, describing the life they lead is almost bound to ask himself how long such a life can go on. Everything in this study bears upon this question and leads to it, so a summary of the central argument may be an appropriate starting-point.

THE HIPPIE LIFE: A SUMMARY

Various social and psychological factors predisposed people to becoming hippies, but such factors were not alone enough. The critical element, in their eyes and in fact, was their passing through a particular process of transformation. This had two elements. It involved, first of all, the relatively rapid break-down of the structure of subjective reality developed through childhood, and then, later—in a period of suspension and disorientation that followed—one or a series of intensified experiences both sensuous and intellectual. About the whole of this experience there may of course have been an element of self-deception. That, I have suggested, was not necessarily important. What was significant was what the hippie *believed,* and the key element in his whole belief structure was the transcendent nature of this original experience.

Subsequent values and behaviour derived from this process. Values and actions must always in some sense derive from experience and be explicable in terms of it, but the relationship is particularly acute in the case of intensified experience, perhaps because of the impression it often leaves of transcending that separation of thought and feeling which a complex society tends to require. The lives of most of my informants were defined at both a conscious and unconscious level by such experiences and by the attempt to preserve and renew them.

In this way, their perceptual image of the social order around them became that of a hollow structure which had to be torn away, just as their own belief systems inherited in childhood were torn away by the beginnings of transformation. This called forth the new theme: an emphasis on spontaneity and directness, an explicit rejection of rules and of formality, of stable and linear relations of any kind. Many of my informants' broad values and attitudes reflected this origin, and it was evident in the whole apparatus of their culture and life-style. In their literature and art it showed itself in the emphasis on psychedelic design, which was symbolic rather than representational, trying to communicate essence rather than appearance; in the persistent use of 'obscenity', intended to disorient the reader and break down his conventional pattern of expectations; and even perhaps in the resurgence in the underground press of comic strips, a literary device which communicated primarily by use of archetypes and essences, making a virtue of tearing away that covering of the particular and individual which we normally think of as making our social personalities.

Their way of life, and the attitudes and values to which it allowed expression, emerged even more fully from the second stage of transformation, the discovery of the New Self. Often it was almost as though the particularly intense experience imprinted itself on the novitiate's brain and long thereafter subconsciously guided him to re-enact it. The re-creation or representation of the original experience, whether derived from drugs or music or whatever, took many forms. What distinguished them was the search for a particular kind of heightened and intensified experience, total and undivided. It marked not only their attitude to time, possessions and people, but also to drugs, to music, to mysticism, to festivals, and to the innumerable other things they might 'get into', and through which these deeper relationships found expression. Each allowed the hippie in some measure to rediscover and extend the original magic of transformation, and to sustain the possibility of that transcendence of dissociated sensibility which it first opened up.

The basic pattern of day-to-day life derived from this. Life became a combination of two apparently incompatible extremes: extended periods of passive receptivity broken by bursts of intensified mental or physical activity. This pattern is the opposite of that characteristic of urban industrial society—a pattern dominated by routine and short-term repetition, which remains, above all, subdued, and which eschews extremity of any kind. Most people's whole life and identity is structured by such roles and routines, so it might to them seem strange that the former pattern could provide any real sense of identity and well-being, but the perceptions, feelings and actions I have described at least raise the possibility. There is some indirect support for it also. E. P. Thompson has suggested (1967) that when men are in control of their own work patterns, their life tends to be characterised by just this combination of extremes—long periods of idleness, interrupted by bursts of intensified activity. Maslow has analysed the general phenomenon of 'peak experiences' and suggested that they may be acute identity experiences (1968). For my informants at least, the original experience of transformation gave a new sense of identity, and subsequent intensified experience periodically renewed it. It was, of course, a rather special sense of identity, being based more on immediate experience and intuition than on the regularities of social behaviour.

Questions whether the one kind of identity is more valid than the other are irrelevant. They are obviously not mutually exclusive; for most people most of the time two such sources of identity may co-exist, however much the demands of a complex social order tend to make that based on social routines and roles ascendent. The people in this book were different. They were at an extreme, concentrating almost entirely on one alternative. Our question, then, is how far an identity based almost entirely on intensified experience made possible a way of life which, in the longer term, they could sustain.

Decay

THE POSSIBILITY OF SURVIVAL

There are two kinds of answer to this question. The first would reject the possibility of permanence by concluding that the function of the culture was to structure a period of transition. It was, it would say, a pattern of behaviour appropriate to situations of uncertainty when the individual could not yet foresee what he would become. In line with this interpretation, we would conclude that none of the people described really thought of themselves as settled into a way of life. The distinctive quality of their culture was that it provided a structure of support, both in values and relationships, for young people whose adolescent identity crisis was unresolved. It provided reassurance by implying that to be in crisis—to have rejected all conventional definition of one's social self—was itself good, a sign of enlightenment. It was supremely tolerant, and thus allowed people to search for their definition of themselves without prejudice. It provided a sense of community, while imposing few demands and no constraining loyalties. The culture of the West End and Ladbroke Grove was, then, essentially a sort of therapeutic community. The only people who could stay in it for long were its guardians and managers, and those too helpless ever to find themselves. According to this interpretation, their values and perceptions could not be a prescription for a way of life: for the crucial values were themselves concerned with the conditions that could enable someone to work through an identity crisis—freedom from commitment, from imposed demands, from guilt at the inability to meet conventional standards; self-acceptance and unconditional acceptance of those around, openness to new experience, rest, relaxation, finding what you enjoy, releasing spontaneous feelings.

On the evidence of this study at least, such an interpretation has much to commend it. The reader will evaluate the lives my informants described in his own way, but I doubt if many will consider that they were the kind anyone could sustain for long. Many informants seemed vaguely to recognise this themselves, and some acknowledged that this was probably a temporary 'stage' in their lives and that they would take such opportunity as arose to move back into a conventional pattern of life. Some

174

sensed that the future would otherwise be uninviting. For a small minority there was always the possibility that success at music or some similar skill would allow them to move back into the dominant society, so to speak on their own terms. But the possibility was slight. In the end, many, even Nick and David, would go back on society's terms. Others, like Jimmy and Ben, would not manage this, and the prospect ahead for them was a series of losing battles with the authority structure of the dominant society. An interpretation of this culture as a kind of therapeutic community thus has some support. The weakness of such an interpretation is its detachment. It sees meaning and significance in terms of longer-term social consequences and social relations. It does not allow sufficiently for the meaning and significance implicit at the time, in the immediate experience and consequent behaviour of the actors involved.

What then is the second kind of answer, and what does it imply? To some extent in conflict with the first, it grows out of the perspective employed in this study. Instead of objective social relations, it depends upon the mental universe and moral outlook of the actors and their particular perception of reality. But it does depend also upon certain facts. It depends upon the fact, which most of my informants attested, that they felt a deeper sense of loss and estrangement when moving in the conventional society than after assuming their hippie identity—however transitory that identity might ultimately prove to be. It depends also on the fact, which they also attested and which nothing can disprove, that they did have an intensified experience which was transcendent at least in the sense that it gave them a new sense of what it was to be alive, and a new sense of themselves and their identity. The divergence is mainly in the point of departure, in the judgment in this instance that, rather than being in an 'identity crisis', the people described did have an intense sense of themselves, and, for a period at least, a stable identity and way of life. The question of how satisfactory and enduring it could be should then be resolved only on its own terms, and not mainly by reference to any functional relationship it might have to the conventional vision of conventional society, or to the normal process of psycho-social development of those who did not become hippies.

This second position is different from the first, at least in emphasis, but the practical conclusions that grow from it are substantially similar: that most of those who become hippies do not keep that identity very long, and that those who do may, by and large, be the losers. But the answer is reached by a different, and, I would suggest, a more valid route than the first. It resides in the essential nature of their own experience, and in the seeds of decay implicit in it. Above all, it resides, we shall see, in its conflict with love, in its dependence on enthusiasm and in the longer-term implications of the repetition of extremity. According to this interpretation their values and perceptions were a prescription for a possible way of life, but one which, through internal contradictions, could not generally be sustained.

Conflict with love: The death of a commune

The people in this book had in common that most of the personal relationships dominating their lives were short and involved no long-term commitment, and often no deep emotion. This, however, was no circumstantial fact: it was a condition of the lives they led. If relationships were open and multivarious, they were almost bound also to be transitory. And here, in its conflict with love, is the first problem of the hippie life.

To explore it, we may follow the history of the commune which Nick described in an earlier chapter and which epitomised the personal values of the hippies. The basis of the commune had been the special relationships developed with the people with whom he had shared his transformation. These relationships were deep and special, but were not like what was to follow. This commune, like many others, was to be short-lived, lasting only about five months. It was destroyed by the fact that Nick fell in love with one of the girls in it. Because of its exclusiveness and permanence, such a relationship could not be sustained within a communal setting. If they had quickly departed, the commune might have continued: but they stayed and the conflict that resulted between the fact of their particular love and the nature of the community gradually destroyed it.

Why did they feel bound to stay? In part, the decision was

the result of group pressure, expressed in terms of shared beliefs: if they left they would just be running away from themselves. It was a penetrating argument, which went to the core of their justification for being in the commune at all: this was, it will be recalled, a belief that in the informal and un-structured relationships of the commune there would be an opportunity to know others, and through this discover them-selves in a way impossible in the formal and structured relation-ships of the cold outside world. A single deeply involving relationship would be a denial of all this. What made the problem particularly acute for Nick was that one of his closest friends was attracted to the same girl. His love would thus become a denial of the bond developed in transformation, in rebelling together and 'blossoming out' together.

So he and his girl-friend stayed. What in the end persuaded them to go was the realisation that if they stayed they would 'ruin everything for the others', by automatically and un-thinkingly undermining the values and goals by which the others were trying to live. Reality to him was embodied in theory in the possibility of transcendent relationships with all who shared the ideals on which the commune was based, but in fact on this single relationship which obscured all the rest. The inconsistency was crippling:

> I was silent for a week. I felt totally confused, trying to follow what I believed. It was like being in a really power-ful car, moving fast but not knowing where we were going. If you try to follow true reality you get yourself into such a state. It took me a week afterwards to find out where my head was.

The experience left Nick deeply depressed. The commune that had once seemed to represent everything that was true freedom came now instead to seem mere escapism. He came to see that one of its attractions had been that it had represented security to him and his friends at a time when they were rejected by many of the people around them. But he was depressed most of all because the relationship forged in transformation was not what it had seemed. He had believed that the intensity of feeling in that friendship had given some material evidence of its truthfulness, and that the reality glimpsed in transformation

was the only sort of reality. His love for his girl-friend revealed
another. In principle there was no reason why the two could
not co-exist, but in fact the nature of the latter undermined the
former. Of the companion of his transformation he would now
only say 'We've gone deadly enemies, I think it's really sad,
really.'

This episode illustrates the problem that. love could pose
when it became singular and enduring. The problem was not
one for Nick alone. Gordon and Annette deserted the hippie
life once the birth of their child gave a new depth and permanence to their relationship, and David agonised for some time
over the choice between the way of life into which he had
grown and an enduring relationship with Georgina. In fact
most of the people we have met were confronted at some point
by the same problem. Many of their values and attitudes conflicted with those of a stable love relationship, and its conditions
even made such a relationship difficult. In Nick's case the
commune and the way of life that went with it became irrelevant,
in so far as they were situations in which he could explore and
discover himself, because he found himself more than anything
else in this particular relationship. So in this way, and in many
ways like it, the pursuit of intensified experience is vulnerable:
the sense of identity it provides could seem inadequate in the
face of other sources of identity, such as that which a stable
love relationship could provide.

THE PROBLEM OF ENTHUSIASM

In a previous chapter we saw another respect in which this way
of life is vulnerable. One of the directions in which the search
for intensified experience found expression was in the commitment to 'doing your own thing', a replacement of routine work
patterns by some particular activity which was important for
the sense of identity it provided. One consequence was that the
hippie life involved a belief in enthusiasm and commitment to
it. While this was in some ways its chief attraction and strength,
it was also a dangerous weakness. Enthusiasm made possible
the autonomous and self-initiated activity which 'doing your
own thing' vaguely represented. It thus gave a new experience
of freedom. But their life not only grew from enthusiasm: it

became in a special sense dependent upon it. To pursue this way of life there had to be some particular 'thing' with which each individual had a sufficient level of identity and involvement for it to give structure and meaning to the rest of his life. The essence of the problem was that such enthusiasms tended to be short-lived. Problems arose when enthusiasm died. To the extent that their life was patterned around the thing of the moment and supported alone by their enthusiasm for it, there was no stable framework which could sustain them in the periods between enthusiasms. In this respect their life was in marked contrast to the life of the 'straight' person, for whom that structure of support is ever-present—except in those rare instances where the transport of enthusiasm may itself take the individual outside it.

Most of the people in this study experienced disorientating losses of enthusiasm. The reader may have sensed this pervasive feeling of loss in the general account in chapter 2. For the people described there it seemed to recur quite often, nagging and biting into their lives. Even John, Nick and Jeremy, who were nearest to their original transformation, and whose transformation was described in most detail, to some extent lost their original enthusiasms, even over the relatively short period of this study. They felt themselves in a kind of limbo. They all wished to recover their belief and their enthusiasm, but there was a doubt as to whether it would be possible. This doubt came even to those whose original enthusiasm had not fully run its course.

This problem must be seen in its proper perspective. For some the loss of enthusiasm was no bad thing. It was a matter of the time and the circumstances. By the time David had lost his enthusiasm he had evolved a more conventional social identity. The loss of his commitment to drug-dealing was therefore of no great importance, although even there sadness showed itself in his awaiting some catastrophe to civilisation which might throw up a new enthusiasm for him. This, however, was not fundamentally important, because his new sense of identity was likely at some point to allow him to move back into conventional society and draw support from it. It might even allow him some new, though more muted, enthusiasms.

Again, there were some few who, like Doug of Federalearth

Freaks, seemed able to recharge their enthusiasm. His experience, if any, suggested that this pattern of activity had the potential to represent an enduring way of life. When one enthusiasm was lost, it was replaced by another; music might now be his 'thing', but previously it had been writing and before that painting. Each had ended with a ritual burning of the books on some seashore when the missionary zeal died, and the times between had to be spent travelling the world anew in search of some new self, but to the extent that several different enthusiasms has taken him through the years, Doug was one of the survivors.

David and Doug were not typical. Most shared a different fate from theirs: that of seeing their original belief and enthusiasm wane, without having anything to put in its place, either by way of a new enthusiasm or of a stable social identity that could survive without transcendent commitments. Like Jeremy and John they felt deeply the transitoriness of enthusiasm. The moments of transcendental experience had to be paid for by the months and the years. For them life became, in Ray's words, a continual search for something to turn them on. For those who lost their enthusiasm without recovering a social identity, and who unlike Doug, could not easily find a new enthusiasm, there was only one solution. They could discover some temporary sense of identity only by returning again and again to the original extreme experience, without enthusiasm and almost without belief. And it was here, in the nature of the repetition of extremity, that the ultimate problem lay.

THE REPETITION OF EXTREMITY

'The Road of Excess leads to the Palace of Wisdom' wrote Blake in a line in *Proverbs of Hell* that has become a slogan. The reader who recalls how Sue and Jimmy, Elaine and Maggie described themselves and their lives should surely feel a doubt. Even if the ultimate condition was wisdom, was it not purchased at too great a price? And was it not a rather unserviceable wisdom that told them little about survival in that conventional world by which they were bound always to be surrounded, but managed only to interpret the special moments and the deeply personal and subjective experiences? No one should deny lightly Nick's own conclusion that he had acquired a certain understanding, but the observer may surely take seriously Nick's own muted doubt, whether in fact the rest did not matter. Wisdom and understanding are rather elusive attributes, but among my informants at least, they were not particularly effective in producing happiness and contentment. Even the joy and elation of original transformation did not long survive.

If observation gives ground for hesitation, so too does more abstract reflection. Few problems are more urgent and important in our society than the need for increased opportunities for intensified experience, and for modes of experience other than that of the everyday routine which can be so demanding and so deadening. All of us live for the special moments. The doubt is whether their magic may not be created by their relationship to those normal and mundane moments to which they give meaning and by contrast with which alone are they special. It is perhaps a matter of the complex inter-dependencies and mutualities that pattern any individual's experience: meditation may sometimes yield a creative flash, but is this not mainly the fruition of ideas sewn previously in disciplined and attentive work?

Issues such as these cannot be resolved, only raised and continually recalled. My question is a more specific one, growing directly out of the lives I have tried to describe and the way it has seemed to me most accurate to interpret them. What was the consequence if occasional intensified experiences became, as they had with most, not just one element in life but its exclusive focus? What was the consequence if a whole way of life was built around the repetition of the extreme experience? Did the experience retain its meaning? Did repetition bring the individual to the goal he was seeking?

I implied in an earlier chapter that part of the value to my informants of intensified experience, of the extreme and critical moments, was that they were—or were felt to be—growth points in their lives. This indeed was the chief reason why they attached deep significance to them. The crucial point is that this value is not one which continues with repetition of the experience. If the experience is intrinsically pleasurable, this alone may be sufficient reason for repetition, but what many comments implied was that after a certain point even pleasure faded. One must conclude that the whole exercise became compulsive and atavistic. The intensification of experience from one occasion to another found at best only quantitative and not also qualitative expression. Most important of all, growth no longer occurred. The hurdle was continually attacked just because it had not been surmounted.

The consequence here becomes the one spoken in *Performance,* a film about some of the kinds of people figuring in this book: 'The only performance that counts is the one that gets to madness.' The reader may want to give that a meaning different from the one the film probably intended, and conclude that the one that gets to madness is the only one that has real significance because it is the only one that is qualitatively different. My informants realised this. By the more clinical and logical, madness was itself rationalised into a goal:

> With LSD I worked out a programme for driving myself to insanity. From my experience with amphetamine, I worked out that if you keep yourself in this sort of ultra, super awareness, which obviously isn't awareness at all, you lose sleep which upsets the balance. It gives you delusions in the end. I figured that about five solid days of tripping would drive me mad.

The preoccupation with madness was pervasive among my informants. The more thoughtful and articulate fortified their position by rejecting the very concept. The books they most often read and referred to approvingly were those of the existential psychologists, and, although they did not perhaps always understand them, they sensed there was food for them there.

In their own terms at least, it is not necessarily an argument against the repetition of intensified experience that it can induce what others might regard as insanity, although many readers will hesitate to give that argument much weight. What is inconsistent and self-defeating is that madness may become indistinguishable from the 'cage' or 'box' from which people felt their original transformation allowed them to escape. It may induce a general numbness of the senses of which Jimmy, stumbling the streets like a zombie, was only an extreme example. The final result then becomes the very opposite of what they sought: a range of experience that is narrowed and diminished.

This was the real problem, as it is for anyone who chooses or is forced to stay on indefinitely in such a culture. A solution to the problem is continually sought, but not easily found. Many aspects of the philosophy they evolved represented an implicit acknowledgment of this. They realised that the pursuit of intensified experience, without enthusiasm, without belief, and above all without growth, might become deadening and self-destructive. There was then one last card left to play. It was to try desperately to pattern their lives on some new notion of 'harmony' and 'balance' which might prevent the road of excess being too self-destructive. The harmony sought was not that 'Bourgeois Harmony' which consisted in holding all the time to the middle line. It was a matter rather of the balancing of extremes. It found expression in the form of mysticism, in fads such as macrobiotic food, and in their private philosophies.

Such a search for harmony was, at one level, what was meant by being a good 'receptacle'. It was always heightened experiences which were sought but it was important also to keep a certain distance from them, to keep them in their place, to maintain a certain balance. The intense experiences might be the route to a real and natural life, but life itself had its own balance and harmony and this had to be honoured. Doug would express this with regard to his particular thing, meditation. He, let us recall, was one of the survivors.

I think meditation is the natural life. It is what your essence is. I feel what we're in now is our unnatural condition and this is a lower consciousness, and when you really get into meditation it's a much higher consciousness. People have the illusion that in meditation you are just sitting there like a vegetable and this is really an erroneous conception because you really are in a super conscious state and your mind and faculties and everything are so fantastically aware and clean. It's like dusting the mirror. You really get into what you are about. Of course, through it you get a lot of revelations and experiences and things that you just can't learn from books or anything else like that. It's like knowledge that you don't get from reading, or from reasoning, it's intuitive. It's not rhyme or reasons. I think the really valuable things in life come from within, come from above and that it's about you're being a good receptacle to take it, and you can't when you're talking and you're riffing and you're playing and you're out on the streets—you're giving out all the time. It's like the tap's open and everything's running out of the tap. When you meditate it's filling it up and you've got the tap turned off. You feel this reservoir recharged, it's fantastic. You come out after a good meditation and it's marvellous, you can cope with everything, you feel great.

The same proportion and harmony was the underlying meaning, too, of the commitment of macrobiotic food which that summer had become very popular: 'Macrobiotic', remarked Maggie, 'is like you don't eat snacks and food through the day, you just have a meal together, and keep it in balance, and try to care for everybody, and try to control all the random elements and try to balance them.'

This conception was sought not just within the individual himself. It was essential also for the individual to be in harmony with the natural order around him. The two were inseparable. It was this realisation which had led Maggie to give up her attempt at inner health and harmony. She felt it was impossible for her to be pure and healthy when the society around her was sick.

These fundamental attitudes found persistent expression. They came more and more to emphasise the organic unity of the individual and the world; it was a matter of the microcosm and the macrocosm. Among the young ones, like Gordon and Elaine, the historical era with which they most readily identified was the Romantic. For others, however, and particularly the older ones, it was the medieval world to which they found themselves increasingly drawn, the world of order and harmony and balance.

For medieval man, that order and harmony was given to the world by the presence of God within it. While much of this book bears testimony to the importance the young people attached to some kind of spiritual experience in their lives, a renewed vision of a God-centred universe was not then open to them. Having repudiated the man-made world and unable to find a god, they came instead to a vision of the organic unity of Man and the World, an evolving synthesis of the two.

Such a vision is in many ways deeply attractive, but it is doubtful whether it provides any real solution to the problems implicit in the pursuit of intensified experience. One may feel, in the first place, that there is about such spiritual doctrines a certain flimsiness and superficiality. From the evidence of the circles in which my informants moved, the doctrines appeared to be adopted and discarded with too great a facility to resolve any fundamental dilemmas. As a mode of spirituality they are somehow rarified and desiccated, lacking the immediate emotional and physical basis which is the real strength and foundation of the kinds of transcendent experience which have been the main concern of this study. Second, the connection with growth has been implicitly discarded, or so at least it seems from the fact that, like other doctrines focusing upon harmony and balance, they conceive the processes of nature and human life as largely circular. It may be that those hippies who espoused these doctrines really did have no more to learn from the kind of intensified experience they had previously sought, that they had sated all their desires and checked out the possible range of experiences. It is more likely, however, that they were implicitly acknowledging the fact that they were repeating experiences without learning from them. In some cases it may also have been that the espousal of such doctrines represented a specific rejection of intensified experience. Each of these is probably one part of a complex explanation, but none of them increase confidence in the viability of the way of life from which they grew.

CONCLUSION

It was not part of the purpose of this study to pass any kind of judgment. The intention was rather to describe and trace the relationships among a particular configuration of behaviour, values and goals. Perhaps the most important question of all, however, is whether they were values that could reasonably be lived by, and goals that had some possibility of fulfilment. The answer to this question is surely doubtful in the extreme. As a matter of fact the espousal of these goals and values was in most cases transitory. But, more important, such transience followed almost automatically from their essential content and direction.

Transience in itself is no bad quality. It does not prove that the values and perceptions were intrinsically wrong. Nor is it to say that the kind of transformation discussed is invalid, and its ideals not worth pursuing. Even those who emerged from the experience somewhat bruised and disillusioned seemed genuinely not to regret the experience. Each in his own way seemed to echo John's conclusion, that then at least he felt alive.

VII

IN CONCLUSION: THE HIPPIE
IN THE WIDER SOCIETY

This final chapter tries to go beyond the study, and the relatively small minorities on which it has focused, to raise some wider questions. First, how do their patterns of thought and behaviour relate to the broad course of change within our society? Second, what kind of response, if any, should it evoke from more conventional people, and from legislators and administrators in particular?

THE WIDER CONTEXT

Where the Flower Power hippies have come and gone, the heads and freaks will probably follow. The moral climate of a society can change rapidly: why should we linger? Rebels who one day appear to be raising issue of critical importance may the next seem jaded and irrelevant. Such a fate may follow as much from success as from failure. Changes in the technical and economic base of a society will throw up new problems more obvious and compelling than the old. Sometimes, too, the mechanisms of instant obsolescence—television, radio and press—can, by endless repetition, turn the revolutionary into the banal. A society's rebels can become in this way its most boring members, and when the majority adopt the outward trappings of their dissent, it can render harmless and obscure everything important in what they were saying. The final irony is that the very trappings of the life-style of the rebellious may be promoted to fashion by the commercial mechanisms of a society dependent on change for stability. When everyone has long hair, when cannabis is the everyday currency of the new leaders of style, what is left? So far as there is an answer to this question it is provided, I think, by three broad aspects of social change on which this study reflects.

The first is that the people described in this study express an important change in the social position of youth, and not necessarily for the good. I referred in the Introduction to their position of relative advantage in income and free time, and to their detachment from many of the constraints of everyday life experienced by their elders. They now also move away in increasing (though still relatively small) numbers from the family home to educational institutions and to parts of London and other major cities which are dominated by unmarried and unattached people of their own age. In the four years up to the summer of 1970 the numbers of full-time students in higher education in Britain rose from 348,000 to 456,000. Those who do not continue to higher education also have greater independence. More of those who do not marry early move out of the family home, living instead within what come progressively to seem colonies of their contemporaries. Such circumstances create the opportunity for them to evolve interests of their own and a culture specific to themselves. It provides the precondition for their becoming, in themselves, a force for social change.

What is happening among youth mirrors what is happening among the old, who by their own choice or others' design confine themselves to age-specific communities, at the smallest the familiar old people's homes, at the largest the whole towns of Florida which have become retirement communities. One of the arguments against such arrangements is they provoke an introverted concern with the preoccupations of the particular age-groups. While the old, removed from normal images of life, sit and discuss among themselves who will be the next to die, the young, more cut off than before from the obvious models of identity a society provides, worry over each other's problems. Increasing numbers of young and old alike may perhaps vegetate in isolation.

It may be that such patterns of segregation by age are a precondition for specifically youth sub-cultures such as that described in this study. At the very least they spread and foster them. They have played a lesser, but not insignificant, part in the very different sub-cultures of mods, rockers and skinheads.

When young people seek out age-specific groups to share their own problems and to create surroundings congenial to resolving them, it is difficult to object. This research repeatedly suggested how easily there could be a circular movement as a result: circumstances made appropriate to the identity problems of youth may simply define and categorise such problems and in consequence consolidate them. What in other circumstances might not have been considered a problem quickly becomes one.

Age-specific social arrangements are more likely to spread than to recede. In so far as the behaviour described in this study was made possible by them, so too will other forms in the future. The quicker that 'hippies' fade, the sooner will they have successors, similar in role and form, however much they differ in detail. This is one reason why hippies must be remembered. Social policy will have to evolve coherent attitudes to age-specific groups whose concerns, interests and attitudes are different from those of the middle-aged majority which customarily dominates our society.

The second reason for the importance of the people I have described reinforces the first. The 'futuristic' writers of the 1940s and 1950s envisaged the world of the 1970s and 1980s as more and more conformist, with less and less cultural and social diversity, and, as both cause and consequence of this, with increasingly authoritarian and centralised political processes. In many ways they could hardly have been more wrong. Post-industrial society, it more and more seems, will be a society of sub-cultures, with different values and preoccupations. (See H. Winthrop (1968); W. Bennis and P. Slater (1968).) The individual has before him a widening range of life-styles, among which he can choose what most attracts him. Techniques such as the computer, rather than enforce conformity, help manage increasing diversity, and in the process foster it. Policies and procedures become more subtle and differentiated as the range of information on which they may be based can be expanded. As affluence creates more free time, so people can follow more varied patterns of living and seek wider varieties of experience. The strange fads and semi-religious creeds that in London are the concern almost exclusively of people on the margins of society, such as my informants, have in California become far less marginal. There is increasingly no 'compact majority', only a steady proliferation of divergent minorities. This then, is the second reason why the people described in this book may be significant for the future, and why policy-makers will have to give more attention to their interests and concerns. The future is likely to hold an increasing number of such sub-cultures and counter-cultures: social policy, whose role in the past has been primarily to foster equality or equity, may increasingly have to learn how to manage diversity and to accept it as a major social value.

The third reason for their importance is that such marginal cultures are often indicators of the future direction of social change. They almost certainly are in this instance. The future of our society is less and less predictable. However great the inertia at the centre of a society and a culture, the range of the *predictable* within them is progressively narrowing. As Peter Drucker has elaborated (1969), the forces of continuity are giving way to those of discontinuity. Many of the attitudes and behaviours which characterised hippies were in one year strange and heretical, only to be widely accepted in the next. This has happened most obviously with styles of dress and appearance, drugs and music, elements which can change quickly. What has happened quickly with them may happen more slowly with fundamental patterns of attitude and behaviour. The numbers of people who pursue, at its extreme, the kind of life described in earlier chapters, will probably always be small. The numbers who come to adopt particular attitudes that the extremists have first espoused will be many times greater. Those who are looking for clues to the fundamental changes in the perception and evaluation of time and routine, work and leisure, spontaneity and play, which may be seeping almost imperceptibly throughout our society, should go to these extreme groups, who will probably be their harbingers.

SOME IMPLICATIONS FOR POLICY

This study was not undertaken with specific policy issues in mind, but it may suggest some general directions which would reward more exploration.

There is a preliminary issue. This book was written in a time of relative economic decline, when the standards of life of significant proportions of the population caused concern, and it will probably be published in one. When our cities, in particular, are the focus of a complex of inter-related and intractable problems of poverty, why should the small minority who are the subject of this study not be ignored, left entirely to their own devices? From many points of view the most desirable policy towards them may be no policy at all, and this is one which they might themselves endorse since they repudiate so many of the values and goals on which policy is generally based. Many would welcome the suggestions that societies should deal with their hippies and the problems they create in much the same way the United States once dealt with the Red Indians: by creating reservations for them, which would both prevent them disrupting the society from which they had opted out and at the same time preserve them from damage at the hands of members of that society. The fate of the Indians may suggest, however, that this is not a very satisfactory solution.

There are in fact two substantial reasons why a policy of total inactivity on such a question is unsatisfactory. The first is that, such is the plight of many of my informants, that there is bound to seem something ethically repugnant in standing aside from it. There is also a more practical consideration, which I regard as the most fundamental implication for social policy: whether or not it is morally and otherwise desirable for a government to ignore drop-out groups such as hippies, it cannot do so because the broad mass of the population will not similarly ignore them. The problem is that it does not require the administrative mechanisms of oppression for a majority to persecute a minority in its midst. It is never so simple. It can be done as effectively by hundreds of thousands of individual people, even unthinkingly, in their glance and speech, in the everyday currency of rejection and exclusion. I have tried to show how such factors helped determine and solidify the particular identity my informants first espoused, often to a degree far greater than they themselves originally wished. Many ordinary people—perhaps from ignorance, mistrust or fear—behave in ways that turn members of minorities into outcasts and pariahs. Some of them were driven, by social disapproval, to become more extreme or more settled in their deviance than they otherwise would. The young people I have described were subject at different times to reactions from more conventional people ranging from unthinking hostility to systematic humiliation. The critical question is whether government should stand aside from this?

It is easier to give a minority certain standards of welfare and amenity than to ensure them fair treatment and respect by others. To do it, if it proves necessary, may in the end require a significant shift in the focus of social policy. This has been concerned, in its most recent stages, to establish national minimum standards of welfare, and subsequently to extend that definition to cover access to a wider range of amenities and advantages, to establish equity across a broad front. Such aims cannot have much importance to hippies, and—if it is true that society is likely to become ever more a collection of fluctuating sub-cultures pursuing independent aims—it may have steadily less importance generally. Much more substantial, then, becomes the role of the State as arbiter, intervening to protect minorities and ensure that other people's fear of their particular difference does not subject them to a generalised victimisation. Some experience of the legislation and mechanisms likely to be more widely required may be available in British race relations legislation. The people in this study could many times have profited from something similar, and an increasing number of minorities may do so in the future. The only way these young people could salvage their self-esteem from the slights of shop assistants, landladies and taxi-drivers, was to lay such behaviour at the door of their unenlightenment, and this was, over a long period, seldom a sufficient support.

None of this is likely to alter the opposite role that the State still often assumes, as an instrument of cultural and social homogeneity. This role is so pervasive, and comes so naturally to it, that it is not likely to diminish seriously. How should it be exercised? There are, I think, two general conclusions on these issues from the preceding chapters. The first concerns the style of debate on such issues, and in particular what is seen to be at stake. The real question with smoking cannabis, for example, is not whether it is intrinsically desirable, but whether the forms it assumes when banned, and the means required to ban it, are more healthy than the prevalence and nature of use likely to result if it was not banned. The substantive issue is often obscured also by the contention which frequently intrudes, that the legalisation of cannabis would somehow imply that 'society' approved of it, in terms of some culture or values to be shared, rather than as a temporarily relevant response to a continuing conflict of values. The contention implies a conception of society different from the one into which we have in fact moved. Some conflicts of evidence and opinion cannot be resolved, but they can be put in perspective.

The second general conclusion is that such legislation, however subtle, is almost invariably only half effective. The victim is never shot dead: he is, so to speak, always wounded in the leg, and shambles around indefinitely causing pain to himself and distress to all who see him (and, incidentally, often placing a burden on social services he did not call on before). When one practice is banned, no more acceptable one is made available. The point is that when particular sub-cultural practices like cannabis and pop festivals are restricted, the effect is generally so to damage the sub-culture that it cannot do those positive things it previously did. The overall result may then be worse. In any case sub-cultural practices seldom do damage to those outside them. The alternatives, then, are either to leave sub-cultures free to *work*, so that they can fill the particular needs of those subscribing to them, and to resolve their own problems; or to cripple them by legislating against core practices, and consequently to create for society as a whole generally insoluble problems.

Those policies which aim to hold the ring and defend the essential integrity of sub-cultural forms from attack by the fearful and panic-stricken can yield other, indirect, advantages. Few of my informants seemed marked by any aggressiveness or particular ill-disposition, and when their attacks upon the dominant social order and its ways were done in anger rather than sorrow, it was generally the result of their having been forced to the wall. In chapter 3 I tried to show how labelling processes help to create hippies, as they help to create most other kinds of deviants. My informants may have felt that they had acquired some transcendent identity, but none of them wanted it to be an exclusive thing. The processes of labelling, by others and by authority, made it so. Having been defined as hippie, my informants were challenged to act as hippie, and often given little alternative but to do so. The result was a vicious circle.

The community and its policy-makers can also harm such people by demanding too soon that they stand up and be counted. I suspect that many of those who appear at various points in this study would have moved quietly back to more conventional attitudes and behaviour had subtle and almost imperceptible pressures to declare where they stood, to stand up and be counted, not made them feel that their previous commitments were now decisive. One of the reasons, I suspect, for the espousal of 'play' as a way of life, quite apart from its intrinsic attractions, is the implication that it is *not serious*, the message to others that the individual does not want to make absolute commitments, and does not want to be constrained into doing so. In a sense, also, such pressures are partly responsible for the prevalence of transformation itself. They create the general expectation that young people should make important choices, rather than drift around not quite committing themselves to anything. It is hardly for society to complain if, when young people like these do make commitments, they are not entirely to its liking.

Most of the people who figure in this study had had rather serious up-bringings. They reflected a persistent theme in our society, the expectation that young people should study hard and work hard, and surrender many of the pleasures of their youth to guarantee in advance the security of their middle age. They were made all too often the repositories of their parents' anxieties about the possibility of downward social mobility. So absolute is this commitment in many cases, that the young person is forced to reply in equally absolute manner: if he does not accept it, or if he fails at it, he feels he must drop out completely.

The absoluteness of such commitments on the part of parents and their governments has generally meant that, at least until recently, society saw only one acceptable path through the educational and social systems of youth. It has not been—and indeed is still not sufficiently—open to young people to leave their schools and colleges for a few months or years and return to them when the time seems ripe. As a consequence the person, like Gordon, expelled from college, must feel the decision final and total: he is in a sense then bound to wish upon himself a transformation that provides some equally total alternative. More flexible educational arrangements may be one part of the solution, but they are likely to come about only when parents cease to take their children's future so desperately seriously.

Such changes may help to keep open lines of communication with young people who involve themselves with experimental life-styles. They may even help to keep some of them, such as David, Gordon and Maggie from getting into the frequently difficult situations in which they often found themselves. On the whole, however, these people are not a social problem, or not a serious one. And their own problems are by no means as severe as those of others. The same cannot be said of the Jimmies and Sues, whose lives are not the product of such seemingly incidental circumstances, and who showed more signs of severe disturbance and distress. Among the groups in which I moved, it was never wholly clear who were the ones who would be able to get by in conventional society and who were those, so bereft of the skills it requires, that they would be destitute outsiders all their days, but that there were many of the latter was quite clear. In so far that such people attach themselves to experimental life-styles, what has so far been said in this chapter is relevant to them. They also pose, however, other problems which are much more serious.

They had often been the victims of disastrous family and social environments; these are things which alterations in public attitudes to the labelling and treatments of outsiders and increasing flexibility in institutions will do little to change. They came to the hippie communities of the metropolis because there was nowhere else to go: any other community made too substantial demands upon them. They contributed little that was positive to the culture I have described, and accepted it partly because it alone accepted them and gave positive approbation to the spontaneous and instinctive behaviour which was almost all they could manage. Extremity can be a therapy, and they sought out the culture of extremity because it alone exorcised their distress.

How does society react to their distress? It does two things, with the best will in the world. In essence it tries to control them and to save them, and so long as it measures only what it set out to do and not what else resulted, it may lay claim to some success. When methylamphetamine was being abused stocks were destroyed by official intervention, with the result that abuse of heroin increased. When heroin abuse increased the response was to limit supply, and one result was increasing injection of barbiturates. When young people slept in the parks the parks were closed, so they walked the streets: when they walked the streets they were moved on: when moved on they had to steal to find money for accommodation. The conclusion I draw is that efforts to control particular practices of a sub-culture will continue to do more harm than good to those controlled (and probably to the wider society) unless they are based on an understanding of the sub-culture and formulated in terms of its needs.

By and large society showed no particular vindictiveness in such attempts at control: they were seen to be both for the general good and for the particular good of the people involved. In its subsequent attempts to save my informants, society was positively well-intentioned. It generally put people already vaguely labelled by those around them into firmly labelled institutions. They were given costly spells of psychiatric treatment or accommodated in clinics and hostels while they underwent cures for their particular addiction or perversity. Because salvation was thought of in terms of a once-for-all solution rather than some kind of permanent support, however, the result was that society had to go on and on, saving them from themselves, often several times a year. For when they came out of their hospitals and clinics, they would return again and again to their old haunts, as David said, because there simply was nowhere else for them to go. This is the core of the problem. With respect to the United States, Marsh Ray clearly showed years ago (1961) why heroin addicts relapse when they leave clinics after cures: the only other people they have been able to get to know are other drug addicts, and the only places they have to go to are their haunts.

The conclusion I draw is that for a number of the people appearing in this book, and for many like them, it is not much use having months of expensive clinical treatment, which in the event only allow them to function in a socially acceptable manner for a short time before the effect wears off. As David was partly saved by his parents at last giving him up, it is possible that the Jimmies and Sues might be saved by society at least half-giving them up. There is little to be lost by putting this possibility to the test.

Some other positive steps are open. We must ask what it was about the communities I have explored that brought people to them, and then see if some at least of these elements could not be reproduced within a different context. Every reader will be able to offer a list of suggestions. These will differ in detail, but they would probably mostly focus on the following: a minimum of structure, absence of commitments and imposed demands, the freedom to search.

For such people what are needed are not temporary centres for goal-oriented treatment, but permanent and communal arrangements always open to them when needed. They must be given space and time for that exploration of themselves and the world in which they are absorbed. The hotels for tourists are no good for them, nor the leaseholds or furnished lettings which suit the more settled. What they need, at least, are those large and anonymous rooming houses where they may stay cheaply a few days or weeks and then move on. In this business there is unlikely to be much profit, so it is probable that government and local authority, or public bodies of some kind, will be needed as landlord. More generally, the building programmes of public authorities may have to reflect the altered family structure of the times, and recognise that the increasing numbers of young people who have moved away from their families have as legitimate rights as the two-child family, and at times almost as urgent.

As important as providing space is the need to provide time. My informants needed opportunities to subsist for a few years, with occasional work that did not involve permanent or even continuous career or job commitment. Many of them warded off strings of personal disasters only through the availability of extremely casual employment. There were a few jobs, such as flat-cleaning, where it was accepted that they would continue only a few weeks. More such jobs need to be created, related to the things they appreciate. They could profit from the chance to tend the parks where they like to sleep, and to clean the squares where they like endlessly to sit. And the older ones, who begin to come through, need the opportunity to contribute the fruits of often painful experience to those who follow by choice or necessity in their footsteps. Many of the people described are bereft of personal resources and more than usually dependent on the public realm. They need the chance to develop, in the least contraining way possible, relationships of reciprocity with it.

NOTES

CHAPTER I INTRODUCTION

1 This study was associated with a larger-scale inquiry reported in M. Young and P. Willmott (1973). See References.
2 According to a small survey by John Neulinger in New York, 95 per cent of respondents gave definitions of leisure couched in terms of time and of activity. Only for the remaining 5 per cent was it expressed in terms with which hippies would sympathise. For the small minority it was expressed in terms of a 'state of mind' or mode of experience.
3 On generations, and their importance, see J. Ortega y Gasset (1959), and the political studies of Marvin Rintala, in particular (1963).
4 The recent sociological literature on political socialisation is extensive. Those who wish to pursue issues only mentioned here may find helpful the detailed references in R. E. Dowse and J. Hughes (1971).
5 See in particular D. Riesman (1958, 1964).
6 For a full description of the sampling procedures and research methods, see Young and Willmott (1973).

CHAPTER II THE LIFE OF THE LONDON HIPPIE

1 These and subsequent figures are drawn from the report on the first year's work for the New Horizon Youth Centre.

CHAPTER III TRANSFORMATION: BECOMING A HIPPIE

1 On this, see in particular E. T. Hall (1959, 1966).
2 Parts of the brief argument in the next few pages lean heavily on the interactionist studies of deviance, led by Howard Becker. The reader who is unfamiliar with this literature and wishes to pursue the matter, is referred initially to Becker's essays (1963) and David Matza (1969).
3 Greil Marcus (ed.), *Rock and Roll Will Stand*, quoted in *Rolling Stone*, 16 January 1970, p. 34.

CHAPTER IV THE WISDOM OF EXCESS

1 For an illuminating psychoanalytical interpretation of time and money, relevant to this study, see N. Brown (1959), particularly chapters 8 and 15.
2 See S. Fisher and R. L. Fisher (1953); R. Knapp (1962); R. Knapp and J. Garbutt (1958); L. LeShan (1952); and J. Roth (1963).

CHAPTER V THE SACRAMENTS OF RENEWAL

1 *The Times*, 1 August 1970.
2 See E. Durkheim (1915), particularly the comments on 'moral remaking', p. 427.

REFERENCES

ADVISORY COMMITTEE ON DRUG DEPENDENCE (1970). *The Amphetamines and Lysergic Acid Diethylamide*, London, HMSO.

BECKER, H. (1963). *Outsiders*. New York, Free Press.

BENNIS, W.G. and SLATER, P.E. (1968). *The Temporary Society*. New York, Harper & Row.

BERGER, B.M. (1971). 'Audiences, art and power', *Transaction*, May, pp. 25–30.

BERGER, P. and LUCKMANN, T. (1967). *The Social Construction of Reality*. London, Allen Lane.

BROWN, N. (1959). *Life Against Death*. London, Routledge & Kegan Paul.

BUTLER, D. and STOKES, D. (1969). *Political Change in Britain*. London, Macmillan.

COHN, N. (1967). *The Pursuit of the Millennium*. London, Secker & Warburg.

DEPARTMENT OF EMPLOYMENT (1971). *British Labour Statistics: Historical Abstract 1886–1968*, London, HMSO.

DOWSE, R. E. and HUGHES, J. (1971). 'The family, the school, and the political socialisation process', *Sociology*, 5(1), pp. 21–45.

DRUCKER, P.F. (1969). *The Age of Discontinuity*. London, Heinemann.

DURKHEIM, E. (1915). *The Elementary Forms of the Religious Life*. London, George Allen & Unwin.

DURKHEIM, E. (1933). *The Division of Labor in Society*. Chicago, Free Press.

ELIADE, M. (1954). *The Myth of the Eternal Return*. London, Routledge & Kegan Paul.

ELIOT, T.S. (1932). 'The Metaphysical Poets', in *Selected Essays*. London, Faber.

ERIKSON, E. (1968). *Identity, Youth and Crisis*. New York, Norton.

FISHER, S. and FISHER, R.L. (1953). 'Unconscious conception of parental figures as a factor influencing perception of time', *Journal of Personality*, 21(4), pp. 496–505.

FOUCAULT, M. (1967). *Madness and Civilisation*. London, Tavistock.

GARBUTT, J. and KNAPP, R. (1958). 'Time imagery and the achievement motive', *Journal of Personality*, 26, pp. 426–34.

GASSET, J. ORTEGA Y (1959). *Man and Crisis*. London, Allen & Unwin.

HALL, E.T. (1959). *The Silent Language*. New York, Doubleday.

HALL, E.T. (1966). *The Hidden Dimension*. New York, Doubleday.

HEITGER, M. (1970). 'The consumer and education', *Knowledge is Power*, International Organisation of Consumers' Unions, pp. 53–60.

KNAPP, R. (1962). 'Attitudes towards time and aesthetic choice', *Journal of Social Psychology*, 56, pp. 79–87.

LESHAN, L. (1952). 'Time orientation and social class', *Journal of Abnormal and Social Psychology*, 47, pp. 589–92.

LINDER, S.B. (1970). *The Harried Leisure Class*. New York, Columbia University Press.

LUBELL, S. (1968). 'That generation gap', *The Public Interest*, 13.

References

MARCUSE, H. (1964). *One-Dimensional Man*. London, Routledge & Kegan Paul.

MARTIN, A.R. (1961). 'Self-alienation and the loss of leisure', *American Journal of Psychoanalysis*, 21, pp. 156–65.

MASLOW, A.H. (1968). *Towards a Psychology of Being*. New York, Van Nostrand Reinhold.

MATTHIESSEN, F.O. (1958). *The Achievement of T.S. Eliot*. New York, Oxford University Press.

MATZA, D. (1969). *Becoming Deviant*. New York, Prentice-Hall.

MAUSS, M. (1969). *The Gift*. London, Cohen & West.

MERTON, R. (1938). 'Social structure and anomie', *American Sociological Review*, 3, October, pp. 672–82.

MERTON, R. (1957). *Social Theory and Social Structure* (revised ed.). Chicago, Free Press.

NEVILLE, R. (1970). *Play Power*. London, Jonathan Cape.

PIEPER, J. (1952). *Leisure, the Basis of Culture*. London, Pantheon Books.

RAY, M.B. (1961). 'Abstinence cycles and heroin addicts', *Social Problems*, 9 (2), pp. 132–40.

RIESMAN, D. (1958). 'Work and leisure in post-industrial society', in *Mass Leisure*, ed. E. Larrabee and R. Meyersohn, Chicago, Free Press.

RIESMAN, D. (1964). *Abundance for What?* London, Chatto & Windus.

RINTALA, M. (1963). 'A generation in politics—a definition', *The Review of Politics*, 25, October, pp. 509–22.

ROTH, J. (1963). *Timetables: Structuring the Passage of Time in Hospital Treatment and Other Careers*. Indianapolis, Bobbs-Merrill.

THOMPSON, E.P. (1967). 'Time, work-discipline and industrial capitalism', *Past and Present*, 38.

WINTHROP, H. (1968). *Ventures in Social Interpretation*. New York, Appleton.

YOUNG, M. and WILLMOTT, P. (1973). *The Symmetrical Family*. London, Routledge & Kegan Paul.

ZINBERG, N.E. (1967). 'Facts and fancies about drug addiction', *The Public Interest*, 6, pp. 75–90.

INDEX

Index

Communes, 57, 85–6, 113–16, 176–8
  and intensified experience, 115–16,
    177
  kinds among hippies, 113–14
  and love, 176–8
  origin and function, 114–16
  and transformation, 115–16
Communities
  age-specific, 188–9
  retirement, 188
Communal support, need for, 197
Crime, sensuality of, 110–11
  see also Theft
Cycles and social roles, 106

Demonstrations, 50
Department of Employment, 20
Deviance, sociology of, 28–9
'Dissociation of sensibility', 38,
  65, 97, 119–20
Division of labour, 10
Downward social mobility, 194
Dowse, R. E., 199
'Do your own thing', 38, 117–20
  meaning to young people, 24–6
Drucker, P., 190
Drug dealers, 41–2, 59, 150–61
  attitude to drugs, 158
  functions for underground,
    158
  initiation, 153–4, 157–8
  motivation, 155–7
  role conflicts of, 159–60
  work, 155–7
Drug use
  categories of, 148–9
  contributory causes, 147–8
  description of effects, 60–4,
    148–50
  initiation to, 143–6
  termination, 145–6
  user's perception of, 144–5
Drugs, 30, 36, 81, 83, 141–61
  economic importance to under-
    ground, 123
  fantasies about, 141–2
  and intensified experience, 86, 96
  and transformation, 142, 143–6

Durkheim, Emile, 11, 199
Durophet, 148
Dylan, Bob, 87

Easy Rider, 9, 109
Educational policy, 194–5
Electric Cinema, 51
Eliade, M., 52, 166
Eliot, T. S., 40, 86, 97, 119
Enthusiasm
  and autonomy, 120
  effects of loss, 179–80
  importance to hippies, 117–20,
    178–9
  limitations, 178–80
  and social change, 137
  transitoriness, 180
Erikson, E., 77
Exchange of goods
  among hippies, 111–12
  in primitive societies, 111
Excitement, *see* Intensified
  experience
Extremity
  culture of, 195
  and madness, 182–3
  repetition of, 180–5
  and search for harmony, 183–4

Family
  conflicts of hippies with, 41–2,
    55, 82, 134
  in contemporary society, 134
  redefined by underground, 134–5
Fisher, R. L., 199
Fisher, S., 199
Florida, 188
Folk music, 4
Foucault, M., 97
'Fourteen Hour Technicolour
  Dream', 162
'Freak', *see* Hippies
Freud, Sigmund, 4, 11, 112
Friendz, 51
Futuristic writers, 189
Fuzz, *see* Hippies, conflicts with
  police

Index

Index

ABOUT THE AUTHOR

Richard Mills read Philosophy, Politics, and Economics at Balliol College, Oxford. In 1967 he joined the Institute of Community Studies in London, where he worked on a study of the London Region before beginning the fieldwork for the present book.